A Guide Through Narnia

Revised and Expanded Edition

Martha C. Sammons

Regent College Publishing
Vancouver, British Columbia

A Guide through Narnia, Revised and Expanded Edition
Copyright © 2004 Martha C. Sammons

Published 2004 by Regent College Publishing
5800 University Blvd., Vancouver, BC V6T 2E4 Canada
www.regentpublishing.com

Original edition published 1979 by Harold Shaw Publishers, Wheaton,
Illinois, as part of the Wheaton College Literary series.

National Library of Canada Cataloguing in Publication Data

Sammons, Martha C., 1949-
        A guide through Narnia / Martha C. Sammons. — 2nd ed.

Includes bibliographical references.
ISBN 1-57383-308-8

    1. Lewis, C. S. (Clive Staples), 1898-1963. Chronicles of Narnia.
    2. Lewis, C. S. (Clive Staples), 1898-1963—Criticism and interpretation.
3. Children—Books and reading—Great Britain—History—20th century.
4. Children's stories, English—History and criticism. 5. Christian fiction,
English—History and criticism. 6. Fantasy fiction, English—History and
criticism. 7. Narnia (Imaginary place) I. Title.

PR6023.E926C537 2004   823'.912   C2004-900906-0

Contents

Acknowledgements

The author gratefully acknowledges the use of excerpts from the following copyrighted material:

from A FAR-OFF COUNTRY, by Martha C. Sammons. Copyright © 2000 by University Press of America.

from THE LION, THE WITCH AND THE WARDROBE, by C. S. Lewis. Copyright © 1950 by Macmillan Publishing Co., Inc. renewed 1978 by Arthur Owen Barfield. Reprinted with permission of Macmillan Publishing Co., Inc. and Collins Publishers.

from THE MAGICIAN'S NEPHEW, by C. S. Lewis. Copyright © 1955 by C. S. Lewis. Reprinted with permission of Macmillan Publishing Co., Inc. and The Bodley Head.

from THE LAST BATTLE, by C. S. Lewis. Copyright © 1956 by C. S. Lewis. Reprinted with permission of Macmillan Publishing Co., Inc. and The Bodley Head.

from THE SILVER CHAIR, by C. S. Lewis. Copyright © 1953 by Macmillan Publishing Co., Inc. Reprinted with permission of Macmillan Publishing Co., Inc. and Collins Publishers.

from PRINCE CASPIAN, by C. S. Lewis. Copyright © 1952 by Macmillan Publishing Co., Inc. Reprinted with permission of Macmillan Publishing Co., Inc. and Collins Publishers.

from THE HORSE AND HIS BOY, by C. S. Lewis. Copyright © 1954 by Macmillan Publishing Co., Inc. Reprinted with permission of Macmillan Publishing Co., Inc. and Collins Publishers.

from THE WEIGHT OF GLORY, by C. S. Lewis. Copyright © 1949 by Macmillan Publishing Co., Inc., renewed 1977 by Arthur Owen Barfield. Reprinted with permission of Macmillan Publishing Co., Inc. and Collins Publishers.

from OF OTHER WORLDS: ESSAYS AND STORIES, by C. S. Lewis, edited by Walter Hooper. Copyright © 1966 by The Executors of the Estate of C. S. Lewis. Reprinted by permission of Harcourt Brace Jovanovich, Inc. and Collins Publishers.

from SURPRISED BY JOY, by C. S. Lewis. Copyright © 1955 by C. S. Lewis. Published by Harcourt Brace Jovanovich. Reprinted by permission of Collins Publishers.

I also gratefully acknowledge the excerpts from "Past Watchful Dragons," by Walter Hooper. Copyright © 1971 by Walter Hooper and the Estate of C. S. Lewis. Published in IMAGINATION AND THE SPIRIT, edited by Charles Huttar. Used by permission from Walter Hooper and Wm. B. Eerdmans Publishing Co.

Acknowledgements Continued

I want to thank:

Rob Clements for asking me to do this project and for his production assistance.

Thomas Georg for permission to use the cover illustration.

Margi and Mardi Sammons for editing assistance.

A special thanks to Clyde S. Kilby, who not only introduced me to the Joy of C. S. Lewis's writing but also to all of literature as well—and most especially the joy of his own wit and wisdom. He undoubtedly is enjoying Aslan's country.

I am also grateful for continual support from my husband, Martin; Marci Sammons; and Dr. and Mrs. Edward J. Cragoe, Jr.

This project was made possible by a sabbatical from Wright State University.

Design and Layout

Cover Illustration:
Thomas Georg
Dipl. Designer AGD

Cover Design and Layout:
Rob Clements

Inside Design and Layout:
Martha C. Sammons

Narnia Timeline:
Martin C. Sammons

Introduction

The purpose of this book is to tell you about the creator of the seven Narnia books, how he came to write them, and to describe their characteristics as "fairy tales" and their effect on readers of these Chronicles.

Published during a relatively brief time—only about six years—the Narnia tales achieved quick success, especially as children read them and their parents eagerly grabbed them up to see what their offspring were so excited about. Lewis's friend, Walter Hooper, tells of a boy in Oxford, for instance, whose parents found him chopping away at the back of their wardrobe and into the bricks of their house, trying to get into Narnia. *The Last Battle* received the Carnegie Medal for the best children's book of 1956.

Estimates are that over 200 million of Lewis's books and 100 million of his Narnia Chronicles have been sold. There have been celebrations honoring the 100th anniversary of Lewis's birthday and the 50th anniversary of *The Lion, the Witch and the Wardrobe*. Names like "Aslan" and "Narnia" are used for everything from company names to music groups. There are Narnia discussion groups that meet in person and on the Web, as well as numerous Web sites and even Puddleglum fan lists. A multitude of products are available, including recipe and trivia books, games, puzzles, paper dolls, calendars, poetry, and jewelry.

Yet these "fairy tales" are not just for children. In fact, these stories have become Lewis's most widely read and best-selling books. Readers range from four-and-a-half year olds to monks, who read them for their theology, to college students analyzing them in depth for college courses and masters' theses. Of all Lewis's works, ranging from literary criticism to Christian apologetics to fiction, many believe the seven Narnia Chronicles to be his best and most lasting works.

C. S. Lewis once wrote that the test of a good book is the number of times you can read it and find more in it than you did to begin with, or to find that your delight doesn't diminish when you re-read it. Although this "test" seems to hold true for all of Lewis's novels, the Narnia tales seem overwhelmingly packed with adventure, suspense, humor and sorrow, philosophy and theology. Of course, Lewis would be the first to urge readers not to "try" to find things they didn't see themselves in these books or have inherently within them to begin with. You may think of them simply as good children's stories or may sense the many virtues the young heroes and heroines learn during their visits.

A unique view of mankind, especially in our modern world, can be seen in four ordinary English children becoming Kings and Queens. Lewis believed in the potential of each individual to some day be a King or Queen of heaven. Eustace is turned into a dragon and literally peeled out of his sins by Aslan. Others like him are turned inside out, their prideful personalities remade by Aslan. Furthermore, each individual learns to obey and to perform his or her particular task when summoned into Aslan's world. This harmonious plan of things is jarred out of tune by evil, which is not only confronted and defeated in a personal, internal warfare but also externally—in perpetual battles with wolves, bad dwarfs, Witches, and the like. By experiencing the effects of evil on Narnia, by learning to recognize the various shapes and disguises of evil, and by perceiving the nature of temptation, we can certainly better understand it in our own world and learn to overcome it.

After reading these stories, you may return to the "real world" changed, with a new way of looking at things, your mind opened to the possibilities of an unseen spiritual world and the limits of merely human intellect and undeveloped imagination. On an even deeper level, though, perhaps you may be touched in a special and personal way by the Great Lion, Aslan himself—and the infinite, bounding joy he brings and bestows on his country, or the terror he evokes in those who fear and hate him. Or you may hear echoes of some Christian concept presented in a startling new way, without its "stained-glass-and-Sunday school associations." No matter what you have enjoyed about these stories, this book will help you understand a little more about the author of the Narnia Chronicles and, more important, about the Creator and Author depicted within its pages, whose Story "no one on earth has read: which goes on for ever: in which every chapter is better than the one before."

This revised and expanded version of the book has been updated to include new information—especially insights provided in Lewis's *Letters to Children*—and new resources.

In addition, the book has been reorganized based on the process Lewis used to write the books as *fairy stories*. Lewis writes, "I wrote fairy tales because the Fairy Tale seemed the ideal Form for the stuff I had to say (*On Stories* 47). This book describes why Lewis chose the fairy form, what "stuff" he had to say, and the effects of this form.

The chapters are as follows:

Seeing Pictures: This chapter describes Lewis's life and conversion and how he came to write the Narnia books.

It also briefly reviews the stories chronologically and summarizes the publication history and other media versions.

Selecting the Ideal Form: This chapter describes the Narnia tales as fairy stories. It explains Lewis's beliefs about why this genre was the best form for his ideas and the appropriate audience. It also outlines fairy tale characteristics in the Narnia tales, such as the secondary world, creation of Narnia, battle between good and evil, magic, history, geography, and talking animals. Finally, it discusses Lewis's method of writing in fairy tale style.

Seeing Man as a Hero: This chapter describes the types of heroes Lewis portrays in the fairy tale tradition. It reviews the primary human characters and the roles of Sons of Adam and Daughters of Eve in Narnia.

Stealing Past Dragons: This chapter describes why Lewis chose the fairy tale format to "suppose" what Christ might be like in another world as a Lion. It describes characteristics of religious fantasy, the difference between allegory and "supposition," and the character of Aslan. It also presents the Christian elements in the books: the creation, tree and garden symbols, temptation, sacrifice and resurrection, salvation, and the end times.

Stepping Through the Door: This chapter focuses on the effects of fantasy: recovery and satisfaction of desires. It describes the themes of longing, dream versus reality, Platonism, desire to escape death, and the consolation of the happy ending, or "Eucatastrophe."

Seeing Pictures 1

"All my seven Narnian books. . . .began with seeing pictures in my head."
On Stories 53

The Creation of the Chronicles

C. S. Lewis—considered one of the most popular and influential Christian apologists—has become well-known as the author of an overwhelmingly varied range of books other than the Narnia tales. He is a well-respected authority on Medieval and Renaissance literature and John Milton; he has written key theological works such as *Miracles* and *The Problem of Pain*; and he wrote a fiction trilogy (*Out of the Silent Planet, Perelandra, That Hideous Strength*). His book *Mere Christianity* was instrumental in the conversion of people as diverse as Charles Colson and Eldridge Cleaver. *The Screwtape Letters* is a unique classic with the devil as the main character advising his nephew on how to corrupt a human soul. The slim volume *The Abolition of Man* has been called one of the great philosophical books of our time. When asked what quality about Lewis impressed them most, members of the New York C. S. Lewis Society gave a wide range of responses, mentioning such qualities as "joy," "truth," "imagination," "wholeness," "belief," "holiness," "light" and "beauty."

But why would a bachelor Professor of Medieval and Renaissance Literature at Cambridge University write seven children's stories when he was in his fifties? While it is always difficult to point categorically to elements of an author's life as influences in his writings, some of the most important events in Lewis's life helped to mold his creative imagination and led to his writing the Narnian Chronicles.

If you are interested in learning more, Lewis's life is described at length by Walter Hooper and Roger Green in *C. S. Lewis: A Biography*, and by Lewis himself in his autobiography, *Surprised By Joy*.

Lewis's Life

Clive Staples Lewis was born on November 29, 1898 in Belfast. (His nickname for himself was Jack). He died on November 22, 1963—the same day John F. Kennedy was assassinated. When his mother died before he was ten, Lewis was very angry at God for not miraculously healing her like a Magician. Perhaps some of his deep distress at his mother's long illness is reflected in Digory's sorrow over his dying mother and her joyous recovery through the life-giving apple from Aslan.

When Lewis was five, his family moved to a huge house called Little Lea with an atmosphere that had a profound influence on him and his older brother, Warren. There were quantities of books stacked in every available nook in the house. Lewis says, "I am a product of long corridors, empty sunlit rooms, distant noises of gurgling cisterns and pipes, and the noise of wind under the tiles" (*Surprised* 10). Because of the typical cold wetness of the climate of Great Britain, the boys were often driven to entertain themselves indoors. One room had a large carved oak wardrobe that his grandfather built. Lewis and Warren sat inside it and told stories. In *The Magician's Nephew*, Digory and Polly explore the attic above their houses just as Lewis did. The cold, wet summer drove them to do "indoor exploration."

Such a setting allowed Lewis's fertile imagination to grow. His nurse told the boys stories of myth and legend. In addition, he was fascinated by Beatrix Potter's books and by animal cartoons. So Lewis began writing his own stories before he was six and up until the time he was 12. He attributes his turn to writing to the fact that he had only one joint in his thumb and thus was clumsy at everything else. So, he tells us in his autobiography, he "staked out a claim to one of the attics" and decorated it with his own pictures or those from magazines. Similarly, Polly Plummer used part of the tunnel beside the cistern as a "smuggler's cave." She brought up pieces of packing cases, broken chairs, and other things to make a floor. She also kept a cash-box filled with treasures and a story she was writing.

Polly's creator, C. S. Lewis, wrote his first stories in this kind of hideaway, too: "Here my first stories were written, and illustrated, with enormous satisfaction." He "wrote about chivalrous mice and rabbits who rode out in complete mail to kill not giants but cats" (*Surprised* 13). His stories were about a medieval country called Animal-Land, inhabited by an array of characters such as Bublish I; a frog, Lord John Big; a horse, Samuel Macgoullah; and an owl, Viscount Puddiphat. A heroic mouse called Peter was another key character in these stories and is perhaps the basis for Peter and Reepicheep. The first book, called *The King's Ring*, centered on the theft of some crown jewels in the reign of Benjamin I. Another book, *The Locked Door*, was written when he was 12, yet it shows a mature style and vocabulary for such a young boy.

There is some evidence that Lewis's brother Warren was also writing his own stories, set in modern India with trains and steamships. Lewis may have decided to combine the two worlds and their inhabitants into a mythical land called Boxen. He became interested in the setting and systematically recorded its 700 year history, then its geography, complete with detailed maps, steamship routes and elaborate illustrations of boats.

Although we can see how these works might have been the embryo of what later would grow into Narnia, Lewis emphasized that none of the Narnian stories or characters was drawn from these childhood tales:

Animal-Land had nothing whatever in common with Narnia except the anthropomorphic beasts. Animal-Land, by its whole quality, excluded the least hint of wonder. . . . My invented world was (for me) of interest, bustle, humour, and character; but there was no poetry, even no romance in it. It was, almost astonishingly prosaic. (*Surprised* 15)

The stories dealt mainly with politics rather than with the more imaginative events and the sense of joy—the "kind of happiness and wonder that makes you serious"—that pervade Narnia.

A second element runs as a thread throughout all of Lewis's life—the search for joy. It began as a series of "aesthetic" experiences scattered through his younger years. Once, Warren made a miniature garden in the lid of a biscuit tin with moss, twigs, and flowers. "That was the first beauty I ever knew. . . . It made me aware of nature . . . as something cool, dewy, fresh, exuberant" (7). Similarly, the low line of the Castlereagh Hills that he could see from his nursery window— perhaps contoured like the mountains of Aslan's country—taught him longing, or *Sehnsucht*. One day he stood beside a flowering currant bush, and the same sensation came over him—"a desire; but desire for what? . . . in a certain sense everything else that had ever happened to me was insignificant in comparison" (16).

Later in his life, an Arthur Rackham illustration from *Siegfried and the Twilight of the Gods* and a line from this retelling of the Norse myth engulfed Lewis in what he described as "Pure Northerness": "a vision of huge, clear spaces hanging above the Atlantic in the endless twilight of Northern summer, remoteness, severity," and he felt a return of the sense of distant joy for which he had long searched. The myth also contained elements he looked for in religion, and he admitted that he loved the god Balder before he loved Christ. Similarly, throughout all the Narnia tales, we can sense the spell of Aslan's country or a glimpse of something no one can quite put his finger on.

But Lewis's life had another side: "I am telling a story of two lives. They have nothing to do with each other" (119). On the one side was the inner, secret world of imagination; on the other, that of the intellect:

> The two hemispheres of my mind were in the sharpest contrast. On the one side a many-islanded sea of poetry and myth; on the other a glib and shallow "rationalism." Nearly all that I loved I believed to be imaginary; nearly all that I believed to be real I thought grim and meaningless. (170)

Part of this other half of Lewis's life can be associated with his strict formal schooling in one boarding school after another. Undertones of his feelings about school are certainly obvious in the Narnia stories. At 11, he attended his first boarding school, dressed in the stiff Eton collar that he came to hate. (Naturally, in Narnia and Aslan's country, not a bit of elastic, flannel, or starch is to be found. Narnians wear simple clothing that feels and smells good). Setting off for school at the start of a new term, he must have felt much like the four gloomy Pevensie children awaiting the train at the station. Lewis's somewhat irrational schoolmaster, "Oldie," flogged the boys liberally and indiscriminately.

At 12, Lewis switched to Campbell College in Belfast, where he was introduced to literature by his teacher "Octie" and read fairy tales, especially enjoying stories about dwarfs. Then, while attending prep school, he ceased to be a Christian.

Up until this time, Lewis viewed God as more or less a "Magician" whom he wished would go away, and he believed in the doctrines of Christianity simply because he feared hell. At Malvern, though, the Matron introduced

Lewis to the spirit world of the occult, where he became further frustrated at trying hard to "feel" something when he prayed.

It was at Malvern College ("Wyvern"), which he attended at 15, where Lewis probably learned the great distaste he showed for the British school system. He was an excellent student, and his teacher, "Smewgy," further nourished his love for literature, including Greek and Roman myth. But Lewis was lonely and miserable at this school. A "tart" or "fagging" system required that all the younger boys wait continually on the older boys and be ready to serve their whims or succumb to pranks like being locked up in a dark, underground room. It was all probably much like the misery Jill and Eustace experience at Experiment House, where they are bullied or "attended to" by "mean," "conceited," "cruel," "sneaky" schoolmates with names like Cholmondely Major, Edith Winterblott, "Spotty" Sorner, and the two "loathesome" Garrett twins. At that time, Lewis felt paradoxically that God did not exist, and he was angry at him for not existing.

Next, he began private study with a tutor, W. T. Kirkpatrick, after whom Kirke the professor in *The Lion, the Witch and the Wardrobe* is perhaps patterned. Kirke, "The Great Knock," further influenced Lewis with his atheistic, positivist logic. Due to Kirke's excellent coaching, Lewis won a scholarship to Oxford. He later became a Fellow of Magdalen College.

Lewis's great love for learning and his endless reading—from Homer and Plato to classical writers to fairy tales—is reflected in the Narnia tales. Patched together out of his vast memory, they contain fragments reminiscent of Malory and the Arthurian tradition; Norse, Celtic, Greek and Arabian myths; and the books of George MacDonald. He was also strongly influenced by children's stories such as Kenneth Grahame's *The Wind in the Willows*,

Lewis Carroll's *Alice in Wonderland,* and Beatrix Potter's *The Tale of Squirrel Nutkin.* He was especially influenced by Edith Nesbit's books, such as *The Amulet* and *Five Children and It.* Many writers have found similarities between her Bastable children and the Pevensies, her use of a wardrobe, her demon-god Nisroch, and other details.

Lewis's Conversion

A combination of events led to Lewis's eventual conversion to Christianity, and he has since become noted as one of its chief apologists. One important influence was undoubtedly that of a group of friends—his brother Warren, J. R. R. Tolkien, Owen Barfield, Hugo Dyson, and others—who gathered regularly to read their manuscripts aloud to each other, then criticize and debate. His friends argued Christian beliefs with Lewis and began to influence his thinking. He was especially flabbergasted when an atheist friend admitted that the historical evidence for Christianity was quite good. Also, all of the authors Lewis especially liked, such as Spenser, Milton, G. K. Chesterton, and even Norse myths, conveyed a certain "religious" quality that others lacked. In fact, Lewis regarded most of his reading as a kind of "trap" for him. George MacDonald's adult fantasy *Phantastes* presented him with the "bright shadow" he later identified as "holiness." Later, MacDonald's children's books greatly inspired Lewis's own writing.

Then Lewis discovered a book by Samuel Alexander called *Space, Time and Deity* in which he read that it was impossible to think about something and experience it simultaneously. This idea showed him that everything he had been searching for all his life and mistaking for joy were merely its by-products, simply pointers signaling with all fingers that they had their source elsewhere. They were only "appearances of the Absolute," of God Himself, in which we all are rooted. So too, all the children discover in Aslan's country their real home, the real Narnia and England of which all others had been only shoddy reflections.

Thus in 1929, a man who had once stubbornly refused to give in, knelt down and reluctantly admitted that God was God. Two years later, when he set out on a trip to Whipsnade Zoo, "I did not believe that Jesus Christ is the Son of God, and when we reached the zoo I did." Aslan's cure had begun.

Writing the Narnia Books

Lewis's creativity started to flourish in earnest after his conversion. How did Lewis come to write his Narnia books? Were they simply written for his god-daughter Lucy Barfield, as he suggests in the dedication letter at the beginning of *The Lion, the Witch and the Wardrobe*? ("I wrote this story for you, but when I began it I had not realized that girls grow quicker than books.") Or was his purpose to entertain children, perhaps in the process teaching them subtle truths about Christianity and Christian virtues?

Paddy Moore was Lewis's closest comrade during World War I. Before his friend died in the war, Lewis had promised him he would look after his mother. So Mrs. Moore stayed at his home in the Kilns. In autumn 1939, some schoolgirls—evacuees from London to escape the bombing —came to spend some time with Mrs. Moore at Lewis's home. Lewis notes that he never appreciated children until the war brought them to him. One of the girls even asked him if there was anything behind his wardrobe.

> "Once there were four children whose names were Peter, Susan, Edmund, and Lucy. This story is about something that happened to them when they were sent away from London during the war because of the air-raids."
>
> *The Lion, the Witch & the Wardrobe*

Lewis wanted to entertain them and noticed that people weren't writing the kinds of imaginative books he wanted. So he decided to write some himself and began making notes for *The Lion, the Witch and the Wardrobe*. Lewis had only this one book in mind, and he says he had no notion of writing any others. A "hazy sequel" only came to mind long after the idea for this book was conceived.

In the first draft of the book, there are four children, but their names are Ann, Martin, Rose, and Peter. Peter was the name of the mouse in Lewis's childhood stories. Lucy was the daughter of his good friend, Owen Barfield. Lewis said he didn't have real children in mind and made up the four Pevensies (*Letters to Children* 51). On the back of another book Lewis wrote was found the original opening to *The Lion*:

> This book is about four children whose names were Ann, Martin, Rose, and Peter. But it is most about Peter who was the youngest. They all had to go away from London suddenly because of the Air Raids, and because Father, who was in the army, had gone off to the War and Mother was doing some kind of war work. They were sent to stay with a relation of Mother's who was a very old Professor who lived by himself in the country. (Hooper, "Narnia" 105-6)

Thus we can see some similarities between the basic plot and events in Lewis's own life at the time.

Lewis says he is not positive what made him, "in a particular year of my life, feel that not only a fairy tale, but a fairy tale addressed to children, was exactly what I must write—or burst" (*On Stories* 37). In several letters, Lewis says all his fiction began with pictures in his head or dreams. Unsure of where these ideas came from, he is certain that all seven of his books began by seeing images:

> The Lion all began with a picture of a Faun carrying an umbrella and parcels in a snowy wood. The picture had been in my mind since I was about 16. Then one day when I was about 40, I said to myself: "Let's try to make a story about it." (*On Stories* 53)

Other pictures he had in his mind were a queen on a sledge and a magnificent lion. Then he had to invent reasons why they should appear in those particular situations, and the ideas began to "bubble up" into story form.

Still, even after he had begun, Lewis says he was unsure of where the book was really going, and he turned to writing some of his theological books. *The Lion* sat thus for 10 years, uncompleted. Then from somewhere,

> suddenly Aslan came bounding into it. I think I had been having a good many dreams of lions about that time. Apart from that, I don't know where the Lion came from or why He came. But once He was there He pulled the whole story together, and soon He pulled the six other Narnian stories in after Him. (*On Stories* 53)

Lewis wrote the Chronicles between 1948 and 1954. During this time, he was also writing his autobiography, *Surprised By Joy*. By the time Lewis's American friend Chad Walsh visited in the summer of 1948, Lewis spoke "vaguely" of completing a children's book that he had begun similar to the writings of E. Nesbit. By March 10, 1949, he read the first two chapters of *The Lion, The Witch and The Wardrobe* to his friend Roger Lancelyn Green, who encouraged him to complete it. So Lewis finished this first book in the Narnia series by the end of the month. Narnia had begun.

Unsure what should come next, Lewis decided to move on to explain how the lamp-post came to be in Narnia. Walter Hooper says that very few original manuscripts of the Narnia tales exist—only some fragments—but they do indicate that Lewis did work on ideas that later found their ways into some of the books or were tossed out with the trash. A good example is his story of Digory and his godmother, Mrs. LeFay, a magician. The "LeFay Fragment" is the abandoned original manuscript of what eventually became *The Magician's Nephew*. (This and other posthumous publications are the subject of some controversy, as described in Kathryn Lindskoog's 1988 book *The C.S. Lewis Hoax*). Then Lewis got a better idea and wanted to see what it would be like to be pulled by magic into a new land.

So what started as a book called *Drawn into Narnia,* then *A Horn in Narnia,* became what we know as *Prince Caspian,* which took about six months to complete. As this book illustrates, the titles of most of the books changed along the way. Lewis had difficulty deciding on titles, and many of them were suggested by his publisher.

Lewis claims the books weren't planned. When he wrote *The Lion,* he didn't know he was going to write any more. When he wrote Prince Caspian as a sequel, he once again didn't think there would be any more books. Likewise, when he finished *The Voyage of the "Dawn Treader,"* he was positive it was the last book. But Lewis found out he was wrong.

By the end of February 1950, the manuscript of *The Voyage of the "Dawn Treader"* was ready. Because Lewis liked his first draft of the story, it came to him quickly and easily. In fact, he wrote it in only three months. He

A Guide Through Narnia

seems to have worked from a brief outline of the book, although it contains some plot fragments that Lewis never used or else incorporated into *Prince Caspian*.

By July, Lewis completed a book first called *Narnia and the North* (then *The Desert Road to Narnia*, *The Horse and the Boy*, *Cor of Archenland*, *The Horse Stole the Boy*, *Over the Border*, *The Horse Bree*), and finally, *The Horse and His Boy*. This book was dedicated to David and Douglas Gresham, who later became his stepsons, and took only about three months to write.

The Silver Chair (originally *Night Under Narnia*, *Gnomes Under Narnia*, *News Under Narnia*, and *The Wild Waste Lands*) soon followed.

The Magician's Nephew came next, now with the characters of both Digory and Polly, and Mrs. LeFay transformed into Andrew's godmother. This book and *The Last Battle* (originally called *The Last King of Narnia* or *Night Falls on Narnia*) were written at the same time.

The series was finished by the end of May 1954. Roger Lancelyn Green suggested the name "The Chronicles of Narnia" for the series. Lewis liked the name, and the publishers used it.

Illustrations

Lewis had considered illustrating *The Lion, the Witch and the Wardrobe* himself. Instead, he chose Pauline Baynes as the illustrator for the series after seeing her illustrations for Tolkien's *Farmer Giles of Ham*. She was commissioned to illustrate the books and drew 350 line drawings. Many letters written from Lewis to Miss Baynes indicate his approval of her pictures—with the exception of the "disproportion" of the children in *The Lion*: "could you possibly pretty them up a little?" Her pictures are based on Lewis's own sketches (of the map of Narnia, the Monopods) or his answers to her questions (about Puddleglum, for example). In fact, Lewis attributed much of the success of his stories to her illustrations.

The various versions of the books issued over the years vary in the numbers of the original illustrations they contain and in the cover illustrations. For example, the first Collier paperbacks in the U.S. are illustrated by Roger Hane and merely adapt the original illustrations. Maps of the lands and oceans are found in various editions of the books; they originally appeared in the British editions of four of the books. The British versions had more illustrations, and they are black and white. Baynes added color to the drawings in 1998, and they appear in new editions from HarperCollins.

Reaction to the Books

As a result of his series, Lewis, unlike many authors, seems to have achieved almost instant success. We can perhaps understand why his friend, J. R. R. Tolkien, who labored over *The Lord of the Rings* and *The Silmarillion* for most of his life, was somewhat critical of the Narnia books. In fact, he criticized the first book so much that Lewis almost never finished it. He thought that they were written too quickly, the religion was too allegorical and the secondary world was inconsistent. In addition, he didn't like the mixture of talking animals, mythology, children, and Father Christmas. Lewis's publisher and some of his friends also tried to discourage Lewis from publishing the books because they thought he would harm his reputation as a serious author.

But Lewis received quantities of fan letters, especially from children who seemed to react naturally to the ideas in the books and mainly to Aslan himself. In fact, they wanted more books. But Lewis felt he had written enough and wanted to stop before everyone was tired of them. Lewis believed he should have explained things like what happened to the party in the woods that the White Witch turned into stone. He thought people would assume Aslan would make everything right. When a little girl wrote to him and asked about this, he said, "I see now I should have said so" (*Letters to Children* 33). Lewis later developed the timeline of Narnian events.

As for the adult readers, Lewis was pleased with those who wanted to know the sources of his ideas. At first, a number of mothers and school mistresses felt the books might frighten children and were too violent. "But," says Lewis, "the real children like it, and I am astonished how some very young ones seem to understand it. I think it frightens some adults, but very few children" (*Letters* 406). He wasn't sure what elements would frighten people, such as the Dark Island (*Letters to Children* 34). Most parents read them to find out what all "the fuss" was about and, according to Walter Hooper, "became converted and pressed them on their friends."

A few days before Lewis died, he met with the series editor, Kaye Webb, to discuss re-editing the books and connecting things that didn't "tie up." For example, *The Magician's Nephew* says that the second son of Frank I became king of Archenland. However, according to Lewis's timeline, in the year 180, Col, the youngest son of Frank V, became King of Archenland. Lewis did make a few changes between the British and American versions of the stories. For example, Maugrim is called Fenris Ulf in the American version. There are also differences in some lines in *The Voyage of the "Dawn Treader"* when the narrator writes about dreams after the group visits the Dark Islands. Lewis believed he had not emphasized the importance of night fears and dreams. However, the British versions from HarperCollins are now the standard.

Order of the Books

The correct order to read the books has caused some controversy. Lewis did not write the books in the order they were published, and portions of the books were written at different times.

DATES OF THE CHRONICLES OF NARNIA			
BOOK	BEGAN	FINISHED	PUBLISHED
The Lion. . .	1939	1949	1950
Prince Caspian	1949	1949	1951
Voyage of the "Dawn Treader"	1949	1950	1952
Silver Chair	1950	1951	1953
Horse & His Boy	1950	1950	1954
Magician's Nephew	1951 (LeFay fragment, 1949)	1954	1955
Last Battle	1952	1953	1956

Lewis *completed* the books in the following order:

- *The Lion, the Witch and the Wardrobe*
- *Prince Caspian*
- *The Voyage of the "Dawn Treader"*
- *The Horse and His Boy*
- *The Silver Chair*
- *The Last Battle*
- *The Magician's Nephew*

However, the following is the order in which the Chronicles were *published* in Great Britain between 1950 and 1956:

- *The Lion, the Witch and the Wardrobe* (1950)
- *Prince Caspian: The Return to Narnia* (1951)
- *The Voyage of the "Dawn Treader"* (1952)
- *The Silver Chair* (1953)
- *The Horse and His Boy* (1954)
- *The Magician's Nephew* (1955)
- *The Last Battle* (1956)

American publisher Macmillan numbered the books using the order in which the books were originally published. Although the Narnia books are numbered in the sequence of their writing, beginning with *The Lion*, the correct *chronological* order of the events narrated is as follows:

- *The Magician's Nephew*
- *The Lion, the Witch and the Wardrobe*
- *The Horse and His Boy*
- *Prince Caspian*
- *The Voyage of the "Dawn Treader"*
- *The Silver Chair*
- *The Last Battle*

When HarperCollins took over publication of the books in America, they used the chronological order based on the recommendation of Lewis's stepson Douglas Gresham.

What is the best order for reading the books? Lewis believed they should be read chronologically. But he also added that the order didn't really matter (*Letters to Children* 68). Many Lewis scholars, however, still argue that the books should be read in the order they were written.

Why are there seven books? There are a couple of unusual theories. According to Lewis scholar Michael

Ward, each Narnia tale corresponds to one of the seven planets of medieval time. *The Lion, the Witch and the Wardrobe* corresponds to Jupiter, *Prince Caspian* to Mars, *The Voyage of the "Dawn Treader"* to the Sun, *The Silver Chair* to the Moon, *The Horse and His Boy* to Mercury, *The Magician's Nephew* to Venus, and *The Last Battle* to Saturn. Ward bases his theory on Lewis's poem "The Planets," his book *The Discarded Image*, and the plot and details in each story. In contrast, Don King believes each book focuses on one of the seven deadly sins.

Summary of the Chronicles and Events

The following brief chronological review of each story includes events between the stories from information provided by Lewis's outline of Narnian history.

The Magician's Nephew

The events in *The Magician's Nephew* take place in 1900. Chronologically, this is the first book of the series because it describes how Narnia was created. The whole adventure begins one day in England when a 12-year-old boy named Digory peers over a wall and meets a little girl named Polly Plummer. One day, they accidentally find themselves in the secret attic study of Digory's eccentric Uncle Andrew, a dabbler in magic. By tricking Polly into touching a special ring he has created out of magic dust, Uncle Andrew sends Polly off into a place called the Wood Between the Worlds.

Bravely deciding to rescue her, Digory follows with another magic ring and two different ones to bring them back. The two children discover that through dozens of small pools in this drowsy, quiet woodland, they can enter various other worlds. Diving into one of the pools, they find themselves in Charn, a dead world where everyone, including Jadis the Witch, is frozen into immobility by means of an enchantment. Digory, insatiably curious, strikes a tiny bell that wakes the Witch. By grabbing hold of Digory, she comes back with them to England—much to the children's dismay.

After causing havoc with Uncle Andrew and his sister, as well as the police and a cabby (English taxi driver), the Witch is yanked back into still another world by Digory and a magic ring. Unfortunately, Polly, Andrew, the Cabby and his horse Strawberry are also transported into this new world of Nothing—nothing, that is, until they hear the voice of a magnificent Lion, who sings life into being and gradually creates a world before their eyes: sun, flowers, grass, beasts. Two of each animal are chosen by the Lion to be Talking Beasts and rule over all the other animals. The Cabby's wife, Helen, is summoned into Narnia, soapsuds still on her arms. She and the Cabby become the first King (Frank) and Queen (Helen) of Narnia, for in that land only humans can rule.

Meanwhile, Digory is sent on the task of getting an apple from a hill far away in the Western Wilds. He is provided with aid from Polly and Strawberry, who has now become Fledge, a Flying Horse. When they arrive at the garden, Digory again encounters Jadis, who tempts him convincingly to eat an apple as she is doing. Digory is certainly hungry and also desperately wishes to take an apple back to his mother to cure her of her illness. Refusing to submit to the witch's enticement, he obediently returns with an apple to Aslan the Lion. From this apple comes the Tree of Protection that guards Narnia against the Witch for many years. Aslan rewards Digory's obedience and patience by presenting him with an apple that wonderfully cures his mother. The seed of this apple grows into a tree in England, from the wood of which Digory later builds a magic wardrobe.

During the years that follow, 40 earth years and 1000 Narnian years pass before humans return to Narnia, and, according to Lewis's outline, several events occur involving surrounding countries. King Frank and Queen Helen's youngest son, Col, leads followers into Archenland, which lies just south of Narnia, and becomes its first king. Then outlaws from Archenland set up a kingdom further south, called Calormen. The Calormenes, in turn, colonize Telmar (to the west of Narnia), but behave so wickedly that Aslan turns them into Dumb Beasts. The Lone Islands in the Great Sea east of Narnia are given to King Gale as his reward for delivering the inhabitants from a dragon. Then, 898 Narnian years after its creation, Jadis returns out of the North, and the long winter begins.

The Lion, the Witch and the Wardrobe

The events in this book take place 1000 Narnian years after the creation of Narnia, or the year 1940 in England. By now, Digory is old professor Kirke, and the four Pevensie children—Peter, Edmund, Susan, and Lucy—come to stay with him to get away from the air-raids in London. One day, Lucy, hiding in the professor's magic wardrobe, accidentally discovers, not the expected back wall of the closet, but the crunch of snow underfoot and lines of dark fir trees ahead of her. She meets a faun, Mr. Tumnus, who explains that this is Narnia, a land where it is always winter and never Christmas because of the reign of the White Witch. When Lucy returns home, however, it is not only the exact same moment as when she entered, but, worse, none of her brothers and sisters believes her story of entering Narnia.

Next, Edmund accidentally enters Narnia through the same wardrobe and unfortunately encounters the Witch herself, who appears to him exceedingly beautiful. Enticing him with Turkish Delight and the promise of being King of Narnia, she convinces him to return, bringing the others with him for her to destroy. For a prophecy says that when four humans gain the throne, her reign will be ended. Edmund returns to the professor's house. But, having become increasingly nasty from his contact with the Witch, he refuses to admit that Lucy was right about Narnia all along.

Finally, all four children enter the wardrobe one day. They discover that Mr. Tumnus has been punished for disobeying the Witch, and a robin leads them to Mr. and Mrs. Beaver, who help them. The Beavers explain that Aslan, King of Narnia and of all the Beasts—the Great Lion himself—is on the move and has returned to Narnia, and all four children experience totally different reactions to his name. Peter, Susan and Lucy decide to hurry to Aslan as soon as possible.

Edmund, however, quietly slips off to find the Witch, only to discover that she seems quite a different person than before. Horrified that Aslan has returned, she wildly sets off in her sledge, dragging with her poor, cold, hungry Edmund. All around them springtime gradually but steadily reverses the frozen enchantment that has paralyzed Narnia for 100 years. Celandines, crocuses, primroses, laburnums, and bluebells all begin to bloom— and in the very same order as they bloom in our own world.

The three children reach Aslan in time to be ensnared in a brief battle in which Peter bravely kills the Witch's chief, Fenris Ulf, (MAUGRIM) and Edmund is rescued. He ashamedly asks forgiveness but, according to the Deep Magic, the law of the Emperor-Over-Sea, he must be killed as a traitor. Aslan offers to be sacrificed instead. Lucy and Susan then watch that terrible scene when Aslan willingly submits himself to the mockery and jests of the Witch's horrible lackeys and is stabbed with a Stone Knife on the great Stone Table.

But Aslan knew that according to a Deeper Magic, if a willing and perfect victim were sacrificed in a traitor's stead, the Witch would not only lose her claim on the individual but also death would start working backwards. While Lucy and Susan are mourning his death, Aslan opens his eyes, leaps from the broken table, and appears to the girls more vibrant and alive than ever, romping joyously with them to the castle. Aslan breathes on every statue of a creature frozen by the Witch and frees them, leading them all in a victorious battle against the Witch and her forces.

Peter becomes High King of Narnia and the three other children, Kings and Queens. They rule in Narnia for 15 Narnian years. During their reign, the next story takes place.

The Horse and His Boy

This person, a boy named Shasta, lives in Calormen with Arsheesh the fisherman. Shasta discovers one day that Arsheesh is not his real father. In fact, he overhears him bargaining to sell him to a Tarkhan, or great lord. He decides to fly to the north to Narnia with the Tarkhan's horse Bree, a Narnian Talking Horse who was stolen from his homeland. In an effort to outrun what they believe are several lions pursuing them, Shasta and Bree overtake Hwin, another Narnian Talking Horse, and her rider Aravis. Aravis is a Calormen "princess" who is also running away to escape a distasteful marriage to an old lord.

To get to Narnia, the group must pass in disguise through the Calormen capital of Tashbaan. Shasta becomes separated from the others when the visiting Narnian King Edmund and Queen Susan mistake him for the Prince Corin. Shasta is taken to their quarters, where he overhears Susan's plot to secretly escape Calormen instead of marrying Rabadash. Shasta comes face-to-face with his look-alike, Corin, who helps him escape. He awaits the others at the designated meeting place, the deserted Tombs of the Ancient Kings outside the city. There, a giant Cat comforts and protects him at night.

Meanwhile, Aravis is aided by an old but silly friend, Lasaraleen, another Calormen "princess." By accident, the two girls overhear Rabadash's plans to win Susan by conquering Archenland and later Narnia. Lasaraleen helps Aravis escape the city, and she and Shasta and their two horses are once again reunited.

Quickly, they begin the tiring and lengthy journey north, over the mountains, the desert, and a valley. During the ride, a Lion snaps at the horses and scratches Aravis on the back. While a Hermit cares for Aravis and the horses, a tired and disheartened Shasta must travel on alone to Archenland and warn King Lune of Rabadash's plans.

He alerts Lune but gets separated for a time from his army. That night, lost on a mountain pass, Shasta is joined by a giant Shadow in the darkness, who explains to him that all along there has been but one Lion. This Lion has protected him, spurred him on to his duty, and even helped a boat bring him to Calormen as a baby. Shasta recognizes the glory of Aslan himself, and refreshed by a tiny stream Aslan provides for him, Shasta sets off in the morning.

He rejoins the battle, though wounded during most of it. Rabadash's army is soundly defeated, and Aslan punishes Rabadash by turning him into a donkey if he strays from Tash's temple. Shasta learns that he is the twin brother of Corin, stolen as a baby because of a prophecy that he would one day save Archenland. He eventually becomes King Cor of Archenland.

One day after they have long been reigning in Narnia, the four Kings and Queens set out to hunt for the White Stag. Upon discovering the very same lamp-post where they entered Narnia, they return home through the wardrobe to find that no time has elapsed since they entered.

Many years after the children leave Narnia, the Telmarines invade and conquer it, and Caspian I becomes King. The Telmarines silence the Talking Beasts and spread false rumors about Aslan and the "Old Narnia." One of Caspian's descendants, Caspian IX, is murdered by his own brother Miraz, who usurps the throne. Caspian X is born, and the story of his attempts to defeat his wicked uncle and restore the Old Narnia is told in the next book.

Prince Caspian

Young Caspian, raised by his uncle Miraz, is told the real story of his past by his tutor, Dr. Cornelius, who is part Dwarf. Caspian runs away to find the Old Narnian Talking Beasts. He meets Trufflehunter the badger, the dwarfs Nikabrik and Trumpkin, and eventually many other Narnian beasts. At the Council of Dancing Lawn, the small army of Narnian creatures plans to make war on Miraz. After minor skirmishes and defeats, Caspian decides to blow the magic horn that will send for help. Though skeptical, Trumpkin offers to journey to Cair Paravel, once the Narnian capital, to await the possible return of the four Kings and Queens.

Thus just one year after the Pevensies had returned to England, they find themselves "pulled" back into Narnia by the blast of Caspian's horn. But they are horrified to find that 1303 years have passed since they were last in Narnia. Trumpkin, on the other hand, cannot believe that these four children are the help they had been awaiting and must be convinced that they are indeed royal material.

As the group travels to the meeting place at Aslan's How, they find that after all these years, the landmarks and terrain of Narnia are so altered that they get lost. Aslan appears to Lucy and points the way, but the rest of the children stubbornly continue in the opposite direction. Naturally, they reach a dead end, barely miss a confrontation with Miraz's forces, and must re-track to where they started. Aslan appears to Lucy once more and, though the others cannot see him, this time they grudgingly follow his leading. One by one, each child begins to see the Great Lion guiding them easily to the How.

Arriving just in time to overhear Nikabrik's plan to call on the Witch for aid, they defeat him and his evil cohorts, a werewolf and a hag, in hand-to-hand combat. Next, Peter challenges Miraz to a duel, and Sopespian and Glozelle, Miraz's lords, dupe their monarch into accepting. The duel culminates in a battle between both armies; Miraz is killed and his army defeated.

Aslan leads a band of joyous revelers (including Bacchus himself) through the villages, celebrating Caspian's restoration to the throne. Then Aslan prepares a doorway in the sky for the Telmarines, who wish to return to their homeland in the South Seas. Peter and Susan sadly learn that they are now too old ever to return to Narnia, and all four children step through the doorway, back into their own world.

The Voyage of the "Dawn Treader"

Three Narnian years and one earth year pass before Lucy and Edmund are called back to Narnia. The two Pevensie children are staying with their unlikable young cousin, Eustace Clarence Scrubb, and one day all three are drawn into a picture on Eustace's wall into Narnia's Eastern Sea and Caspian's ship, the "Dawn Treader." Caspian, they learn, is setting out for the Eastern Islands to find seven of his father's lost lords. Long before, they were sent off by his evil uncle, Miraz, on a voyage of exploration. On the journey too is Reepicheep, King of the Talking Mice and most valiant of the beasts of Narnia. He is seeking Aslan's country at the End of the World. Although Eustace is miserably seasick and indignant at the whole affair, the Pevensie children eagerly anticipate a new adventure.

Their first stop after several days of sailing is the island of Felimath, where they find the first lost lord, Lord Bern. Felimath is one of the Lone Islands, and although Lewis hints that he would like to tell their story in another book, we learn no more about them. The children are captured by slave traders, but Caspian is bought by Lord Bern, who, on learning Caspian is Narnia's king, helps them plan their escape. Felimath is ruled by an incompetent and bumbling man named Gumpas, the stereotypical politician who sticks solely to statistics, graphs, and appointments on his calendar. By feigning to have an entire fleet of forces, Caspian overthrows Gumpas and declares Lord Bern ruler of the Lone Islands.

After nearly three weeks on Felimath, the little company leaves to continue its mission. Twenty-six days later, badly damaged by a storm, the ship and its crew find haven on an island that they dub Dragon Island. To escape work, Eustace wanders off and comes upon a dying dragon. But Eustace, who has read all the wrong books, has no idea what the creature is. Taking shelter in the dragon's cave, Eustace discovers a cache of magnificent treasures and, after slipping a bracelet on his arm and cramming his pockets full of precious things, he falls asleep. But when he awakens, feeling not quite himself, he finds he is walking on all fours and breathing smoke. Peering into a stream, he discovers he has turned into a dragon.

When the others figure out what has happened, they find their cousin's plight has much improved him, causing him to become more helpful and reasonable. Then one night, Aslan appears and orders Eustace to follow him. After Eustace unsuccessfully attempts to remove his skin by shedding it like a banana peel, Aslan tears off the last layer of painful scales and bathes him in a clear pool, restoring him to true boyhood. Thereafter, Eustace's behavior is markedly changed. The children deduce that Lord Octesian was probably the other dragon or had been destroyed by the dragon.

After the "Dawn Treader" visits Burnt Island (which has been ravaged by fire) the crew battles a fearful Sea Serpent that almost engulfs the ship. Five days of sailing bring them to Deathwater Island, where the crew discovers a pool that turns anything dropped in it to gold. Lord Restimar, they realize, must have bathed in this water and been turned into a gold "statue." When they begin to quarrel over the great possibilities of capitalizing on the wealth this magic pool would give, Aslan sternly appears to bring them to their senses.

On the next island, the Island of the Voices, Lucy is asked by the Dufflepuds, strange creatures who hop around on one umbrella-like foot, to find a spell to make them visible. To accomplish this, she must go into a Magician's House and read his Magic Book. Among other things, Lucy finds a spell to make herself beautiful; a wonderful story about a cup, sword and green hill; and a spell to let her know what her friends think of her. When Lucy says this spell, Aslan appears to her. He introduces her to the Magician, and the invisible Dufflepuds turn into visible Monopods.

Then, for thirteen days they sail for the Dark Island where nightmarish dreams come true. There, the group discovers haggard and white-haired Lord Rhoop, and Aslan appears as an albatross to guide them out.

At World's End Island, the group finds the last three of the lost lords—Revilian, Argoz and Mavramorn—sleeping at a sumptuous banquet table. They also meet Ramandu, a "retired" star, and his beautiful daughter. This is Aslan's Table where the food, renewed daily, is served for those who travel this far. The three lords had quarreled over the sacred Stone Knife (once used by the White Witch to stab Aslan). At the moment they touched it, they had been cast into an enchanted sleep.

All but one sailor set off for the End of the World. The light grows brighter and brighter; the sea grows smoother and white with lilies. The water, clear and luminous like "drinkable light," keeps the group nourished and unwearied. Quivering with excitement, Reepicheep sails off alone to Aslan's country. Now, after a year of travelling, Caspian regretfully decides to turn back with the ship to Narnia. The three children meet Aslan, who appears to them first as a Lamb, then a Lion. He promises that they can come to his land from all worlds and will know him even better in their own. Through a rip in the sky, they return to Cambridge. Thus ends Lucy's and Edmund's last adventure in Narnia.

Caspian returns to Narnia to marry Ramandu's daughter three years after his voyage. Fifteen years later a son, Rilian, is born. One day, as Ramandu's daughter is riding in Narnia, she stops to rest. A Green Serpent stings her, and she dies. Twenty year-old Rilian sets off to avenge her death and, entranced by a beautiful lady dressed in green, is not heard from again, though many seek for him. Ten years later, Eustace and his schoolmate Jill Pole are called into Narnia to find Rilian.

The Silver Chair

Although it is still 1942, the year of the "Dawn Treader" voyage, 50 Narnian years have now passed since Eustace visited Narnia. Miserably unhappy and desperate to leave their school, Experiment House, Jill and Eustace enter Narnia through a gate in the wall. They find themselves high on a precipice in Aslan's country, overlooking all of Narnia. After Eustace accidentally tumbles off the cliff and floats away, Jill finds herself alone with Aslan. Their task, she learns, is to find the lost Rilian, which they will accomplish only if they obey four "Signs." First, they will meet an old, dear friend whom they must greet if they are to receive help. Then they must journey from Narnia north to a ruined giant city where they will find writing on a stone. They must do what it says. They will recognize Prince Rilian because he will be the first person who asks them to do something in Aslan's name. Jill is then blown softly on Aslan's sweet breath to Narnia, where she rejoins Eustace.

Caspian, now 66 and thus unrecognizable by Eustace, is preparing to sail to Terebinthia in hopes of finding Aslan and seeking his advice. Glimfeather the Owl carries the children first to Cair Paravel, then to a Parliament of Owls, where they are briefed on Rilian's story. They then travel North to the swampy home of a gloomy, lanky, frog-like creature named Puddleglum, a Marshwiggle, who becomes a member of their team.

On their mission of search and rescue, the three head north to Ettinsmoor, the land of the giants. A lovely lady, the Lady of the Green Kirtle, who is accompanied by an armored knight, advises them to press on to the giant city of Harfang to receive food and shelter. Against Puddleglum's better judgment, the children desperately insist on finding the city to get relief from the bitter, snowy cold. Through a series of ruins and trenches, they reach the castle, where they are welcomed, fed and bathed. Aslan appears to Jill in a dream and shows her the inscription UNDER ME written outside on the ruins. When the three discover that the giants mean to have them as the main course of their Autumn Feast, they slip through a crack in the ruins—the third Sign. They now realize they have muffed the first three Signs.

Beneath the earth, they descend through tunnel after dark tunnel into a strange land, where they see the varied faces of Earthmen who sadly and silently labor in the city. Among a variety of creatures, they even see Father Time himself sleeping until the world's end. They are taken to the castle of a Green Witch, who is the cruel ruler of this country called the Shallow-Lands. In her castle also lives a knight (Rilian himself) whom the witch has charmed into believing she is a beautiful and benevolent ruler. She bewitches Rilian into thinking she has saved him from a thousand dangers and cares for him most tenderly. He is well content to obey the counsel of the Lady, whom he thinks will one day be his Queen. For she has promised him he will be King of Overland once the Earthmen dig through to the surface. During one hour of every day, however, he is under a spell by which he becomes enraged and supposedly is transformed into a serpent. Daily, during this hour, the Witch binds him to a silver chair. The children fearfully watch as the awful change comes over him—and then he bids them in Aslan's name to free him. Recognizing the last Sign, as well as the danger of obeying it, the three nevertheless unbind the Prince, who destroys the awful chair.

The Witch returns to discover what has been done and causes a drowsy smoke and music to fill the room, enchanting them into believing there is no other world but hers. But stout-hearted Puddleglum stamps out the fire and, after renouncing her world, leads Rilian into killing the Witch as she turns into a snake.

Noisy fireworks signal the Earthmen's glee at the end of the Witch's hold over them. Golg, a gnome, explains that beneath the Witch's land is the Really Deep Land of Bism, inhabited by gnomes and salamanders—a fiery world of live gems and a delicious smell. The gnomes dive into that realm through a crack before a shift in the earth closes it forever.

Through one of the tunnels to the Overworld, the four escape the Witch's Realm to discover that they are back in Narnia itself. They are rescued by dwarfs performing the Great Snow Dance. Riding on centaurs, the children arrive in time to see Rilian greeting his sick father's returning ship. Although Caspian dies, the children are taken to Aslan's country where, on Aslan's Mountain, they witness Caspian's restoration to life with a drop of blood from the great Lion's paw. Promising that some day they too will return to stay forever, Aslan leads them triumphantly back to their school. There he terrifies the children and Headmistress so badly that there is a grand shake-up, and Experiment House ends up as a much better school.

Other than the uprising of outlaws in Lantern Waste and the building of towers to guard the region, we know little of the 199 years of Narnian history between *The Silver Chair* and the final book.

The Last Battle

During the final days of Narnia, Shift the Ape, who lives near Lantern Waste, finds a lion's skin in the water. He convinces his poor, gullible donkey follower Puzzle to put it on and pose as Aslan. Then he spreads false rumors that Aslan has returned and aggressively demanded changes in Narnia: trees felled, Talking Animals driven to work, dwarfs and animals sold as slaves to the Calormenes. The Narnians begin to believe that Aslan is not at all like the Lion they have heard about in stories and legends.

Meanwhile, King Tirian of Narnia, seventh in descent from Rilian, and his dear friend Jewel the Unicorn hear of all these changes and believe them to be lies. Tirian angrily murders two Calormenes and is captured. Desperate and only half-believing that the changes are from Aslan, he calls for help from the past Kings and Queens. In a dream, he sees all seven "friends" of Narnia—Digory and Polly (now in their sixties), Peter, Edmund, Lucy, Jill and Eustace —eating around a table. Immediately, Jill and Eustace (now teenagers) appear before him, rescuing not only Tirian, but Jewel and Puzzle as well.

During this time, much has happened on earth: Digory and Polly, feeling that they are somehow "needed" in Narnia, hold a sort of "reunion" for all who have been to Narnia. Peter and Edmund are sent to London to dig up the magic rings Digory used many years ago to first enter Narnia. They are scheduled to meet the train to hand them over. Jill, Eustace, Digory, Polly, Lucy, and, it so happens, Mr. and Mrs. Pevensie, all go on the same train. It crashes at the station, killing all of them, as well as Peter and Edmund. At that moment (nearly one earth week after seeing Tirian), Aslan brings Jill and Eustace into Narnia "in his own way."

Tirian and the children optimistically determine to explain the ape's deception to the Narnians and restore the old order. However, all dwarfs except Poggin bitterly refuse to believe in anything but themselves. After Tirian's group sees the nightmarish, birdlike Calormen god, Tash, flying toward Shift's camp, they plan to join forces with a few loyal Narnians led by Roonwit, the centaur. A Calormene arrow kills Roonwit, and the enemy takes over Cair Paravel. Thus the children hurry to Shift's camp, hoping to reveal the truth to the Narnians.

They find that Shift has set up a Stable where the Narnians gather at night by a giant bonfire. His new cohorts, Rishda the Calormen captain and Ginger the Cat, have now convinced the Narnians that Aslan and Tash are the same. Ginger and the Ape frustrate all their hopes of unmasking the imposter by telling the Narnians that there is a donkey loose, masquerading as Aslan. Ginger the Cat cockily enters the Stable expecting to find nothing, but instead finds Tash and shoots out again, terrified and speechless. This event, of course, fulfills Aslan's prophecy (given many years earlier when Narnia was created) that Talking Beasts would return to Dumb Beasts if they chose evil. A Calormen named Emeth bravely goes in next in hopes of meeting Tash and never returns.

The real battle then begins. While the dogs and moles join Tirian's side, the dwarfs fight for themselves. In vast confusion as the enemy presses in on them, Eustace is hurled into the Stable, followed by all eleven dwarfs, Rishda (taken by Tash), and Tirian. But instead of finding the fearful god Tash in the Stable, as he had feared, Tirian sees the seven glorious Kings and Queens of

Narnia and Aslan himself standing before him. Beyond the Stable door he has entered a luscious, green and fragrant country. The dwarfs, however, see only darkness, hear Aslan's voice as an angry snarl, and taste rotten food instead of the sumptuous banquet he spreads for them.

Aslan shows all the Kings and Queens that Narnia, on the other side of the Stable Door, is ending. First, Father Time is called to blow his horn, and the living stars fall gleaming to the ground. Next, all the animals stream to Aslan and either pass through the Door if they love him, or to his left and into his Shadow if they fear him. Giant dragons and lizards then devour the vegetation, and the sea rises to cover it all. The sun and moon turn red, flame into each other, and Father Time squeezes the burning ball like an orange until all is dark. Finally, Peter locks the door on Narnia—icy, cold and void.

Aslan then leads them "further up and further in" through the Stable Door to his own country. There they find not only the fragrant green land they had always longed for and discover their own bodies to be full of life and vigor, but they also see all the old friends they had ever known or heard about. Susan, however, is not among them for she is "no longer a friend of Narnia." On the other hand, Emeth the Calormen is there, for he had always sought the truth.

They scale the Great Waterfall and enter the golden gates of a garden with a tree at its center. Far below, Narnia and England stretch out like spurs jutting off from the mountains of Aslan's country. But they are the real Narnia and England; those that they had known before were only imitations. The children are now ready to begin the Great Story Lucy had once read about in the Magician's Magic Book, a story that goes on forever.

A Guide Through Narnia

Other Versions and Resources

The Narnia books were originally published in London as hardbacks, and the first British paperbacks were published by Penguin books as Puffin Books. Eventually, the books were published by Willliam Collins & Sons in both hardback and paperback versions. There have been numerous special editions of *The Lion, the Witch and the Wardrobe.*

In the 1950s, Macmillan published the books in the United States as hardbacks. Macmillan also published the books as paperbacks in 1970 as Collier Books.

HarperCollins became the publishers of the hardback, paperback, and mass market versions of the books beginning in 1990s. In 2001, there was a false rumor that HarperCollins would remove all Christian references in their new Narnia books and merchandise.

The Chronicles are now available in one-volume versions: a hardcover full-color version celebrating the 100th anniversary of Lewis's birth and an "adult" one-volume paperback version.

There have been several film and television adaptations. They began with a black-and-white version of *The Lion* in 1967. Between 1989 and 1991, the BBC filmed a television series version of only four of the books: *The Lion, the Witch and the Wardrobe, Prince Caspian, The Voyage of the "Dawn Treader,"* and *The Silver Chair.*

Disney has struck a deal with Denver billionaire Philip Anschutz' Walden Media to co-finance and distribute *The Chronicles of Narnia: The Lion, the Witch and the Wardrobe.* The film is scheduled to begin shooting in the summer of 2004, with Andrew Adamson as director, who also directed *Shrek.* The film will be released at Christmas 2005 by Walt Disney Pictures. Disney retains the option to release future films in the series, according to Walt Disney Studios chairman Dick Cook. Ann Peacock wrote the first draft of the script, with revisions by Adamson and Christopher Markus and Stephen McFeely. *The Lion, the Witch and the Wardrobe* is the first installment of Walden's planned "Chronicles of Narnia" franchise.

FILM VERSIONS			
NAME	TYPE	PRODUCER	DATE
The Lion, the Witch and the Wardrobe	Live action TV	ABC Television Network	UK 1967
	Animated TV	Episcopal Radio-TV Foundation and The Children's Television Workshop	CBS 1976
	Live action and animation	BBC	1988
Prince Caspian	Live action and animation	BBC	1989
The Voyage of the "Dawn Treader"	Live action and animation	BBC	1989
The Silver Chair	Live action and animation	BBC	1990

There have also been recordings of the stories. The first dramatization, which Lewis approved, was *The Lion, the Witch and the Wardrobe* by Lance Sieveking. It was broadcast during the BBC Home Service Children's Hour in 1959. The BBC Radio broadcast dramatizations by Brian Sibley in 1988. Single-voice recordings of the Chronicles were produced between 1978 and 1981 by Caedmon. They were issued first as records, then cassette.

In 1995, HarperAudio issued *The Chronicles of Narnia* boxed set, *Selections from The Chronicles of Narnia* boxed set, and *The Lion, the Witch and the Wardrobe*. In 1980, HarperCollins of London released records (and then cassettes) of the Academy Studios recording of all seven stories. Focus on the Family Radio Theatre produced all seven of the stories. Douglas Gresham, Lewis's stepson, hosted the production. Each story is 100-180 minutes in length and available on audiocassettes or CDs.

The Lion, the Witch and the Wardrobe has been a popular children's musical. In celebration of the 100-year anniversary, the Royal Shakespeare Company performed a dramatic version of the book. There have been stage and play adaptations of *The Horse and His Boy, The Magician's Nephew,* and *The Voyage of the "Dawn Treader,"* as well as a musical called *Narnia* (published by The Dramatic Publishing Company).

Five "Choose Your Own Adventure" books were published in the 1980s. These Narnia Solo Games were based on the Chronicles. They included *The Sorceress and the Book of Spells, Return of the White Witch, Return to Deathwater, The Lost Crowns of Cair Paravel,* and *Leap of the Lion.*

There have been board games and three video games based on the Chronicles. One board game called "Narnia" was based on the BBC movies. There was also a board game for *The Lion, Prince Caspian,* and *The Voyage of the "Dawn Treader."* The video games were for the Commodore and Apple II computers. In fall 2005, Buena Vista Games, Inc. will publish video games based on *The Lion, the Witch and the Wardrobe* for the PlayStation 2, Xbox, GameCube, PC and handheld consoles. The action-adventure series, which will be published under the Disney Interactive label, will be the first multi-platform video games.

Selecting the Ideal Form
2

*"I wrote fairy tales because the Fairy Tale seemed
the ideal Form for the stuff I had to say."*
Of Other Worlds 37

Fairy Tales

Lewis says he "turned to fairy tales because that seemed the form which certain ideas and images in my mind seemed to demand" (*Letters* 506). In his letters, but especially in the essays collected in *On Stories and Other Essays on Literature,* Lewis presents some of his views on fairy tales and writing for children. He also refers to Tolkien's essay "On Fairy Stories," which he calls one of the most significant works on the subject.

Lewis suggests that a writer chooses a certain Form that determines the shape or pattern of events and the work's effect. Lewis wanted a form that would bridge the gap between the supernatural and the realm of experience. The fairy tale was the genre best fitted for what he wanted to say—the "ideal Form" that his ideas demanded.

According to Lewis, the fairy tale form has several distinct advantages:

- Can be brief, by both permitting and compelling the author to leave things out.
- Requires a limited vocabulary, little description, and chapters of equal length.
- Cannot be analyzed.
- Cuts down on reflective, expository, digressive, and descriptive passages.
- Concentrates on action and conversation.
- Can be both general and concrete.
- Makes experience palpable.
- Gives new experiences.
- Adds to life.
- Is flexible and traditional.

Some object that fairy tales give children false impressions of the world. However, Lewis believes that it is realistic stories that are confusing and improbable because they may give the reader false expectations about real life. Such stories are "contrived to put across some social or ethical or religious or anti-religious 'comment on life'" (*Experiment* 68). In contrast, no reader expects life to be like fairy stories.

Audience

Fairy stories are not written just for children. A good children's story, says Lewis, should not be written "down" as if told to a child. Instead, the author should use the same rules to write for either adults or younger audiences and should speak to his reader simply as one person speaking to another. A good work should also not be written for one audience because only poor stories are enjoyed just by children. Lewis explains that when his imagination led him to write the Narnia tales, he did not begin by first asking what children want and then trying to dish it out to them or by treating them like a distance and inferior race (*On Stories* 51).

In Lewis's opinion, such an approach results in what he considered "bad" children's literature. Only bad stories are enjoyed just by children: "No book is really worth reading at the age of ten which is not equally (and often far more) worth reading at the age of fifty—except, of course, books of information" (*On Stories* 14). The only reason most fairy tales unfortunately "gravitated" to the nursery is because their elders ceased to like them.

The association of fairy tales with children was thus an accident. Lewis says when he was ten, he read fairy tales in secret and would have been ashamed if he had been caught. But when he was 50, he read them openly: "When

> "Even in this world, of course, it is the stupidest children who are most childish and the stupidest grown-ups who are most grown-up."
>
> *The Silver Chair*

I became a man I put away childish things, including the fear of childishness and the desire to be very grown up" (*On Stories* 34). In a sense, we grow through stages when we are first attracted to fairy tales, then ashamed of reading them, and finally perhaps return to them as adults. In fact, the Chronicles themselves have been called one of the very few sets of books that should be read three times: in childhood, early adulthood, and late in life.

In the dedication to Lucy Barfield in *The Lion, the Witch and the Wardrobe,* Lewis wrote, "Some day you will be old enough to start reading fairy tales again." Even Lewis as narrator identifies with this childlike vision when he says Miraz talks in that tiresome way grown-ups have. Near the End of the World, the children notice that "though they had felt—and been—very grown up on the *Dawn Treader,* they now felt just the opposite." When the children are too old, Aslan tells them they cannot return to Narnia.

According to G. K. Chesterton, it is really adults who need fairy tales, not children, for children still have a sense of awe and wonder at the world simply as it is. Most of the adults in the Narnia books are practical, close-minded, and have uninteresting explanations for things. Lewis agrees with Tolkien's assertions in his significant essay "On Fairy Stories" that fantasy can give us "recovery"—a cleansing of our vision of the world, thereby strengthening our relish for real life.

George MacDonald wrote not for children but rather for the "childlike, whether of five, or fifty, or seventy-five" ("Fantastic" 25). In reading MacDonald's *Phantastes*, Lewis found a work that did not make the real world seem dull. Instead, the "bright shadow" came into the real world and transformed common things (*Surprised* 180-1). Lewis says fairy land gives the actual world "a new dimension of depth" and sends us back to the real world with renewed pleasure, awe, and satisfaction. In discussing Tolkien's works, Lewis says the value of the myth is that it takes things we know and removes the "veil of familiarity." "The boy does not despise real woods because he has read of enchanted woods," writes Lewis; "the reading makes all real woods a little enchanted" (*On Stories* 38). For example, child enjoys cold meat by pretending he has killed a buffalo with a bow and arrow.

A theme running throughout the Narnia books is the importance of reading the right kinds of books, such as those that feed the imagination and contain adventure. In contrast, adults like Miraz consider fairy tales impractical or old wives tales. Children like Eustace read the wrong kinds of books or, like Shasta, no books at all.

Certainly, no one of the children returns from Narnia to earth unchanged. Polly, for example, notes how the mysterious tunnels in her house seem tame after sojourning in Charn. Eustace, of course, is inwardly turned around. Through reading, we too learn not to treat things as mere objects, as Ramandu teaches: "Even in your world that is not what a star is but only what it is made of."

An interesting turnabout of this "renewed vision" comes about in *The Voyage of the "Dawn Treader,"* when Caspian is amazed to hear that the children come from a round world. He had only read about them in fairy tales. "But I've always wished there were and I've always longed to live in one. . . . It must be exciting to live on a thing like a ball." "There's nothing particularly exciting about a round world when you're there," says Edmund.

Secondary World

The most important characteristic of secondary world fantasy is the creation of another world that is often more real than our own. In "On Fairy Stories," Tolkien calls this world "*Faerie*, the state in which fairies have their being." He distinguishes fairy story from traveler's tales, dreams used to explain marvels, and best fables.

Lewis describes several advantages of secondary world fantasy. First, fiction containing another planet, parallel universe, or earth in the distant past or future is good for spiritual adventures because such books satisfy the craving of our imaginations, suggest "otherness," and convey "wonder, beauty, and suggestiveness" (*On Stories* 64). Because our world is already known, it is difficult to describe "marvels." Thus faerie lets us search for the "beauty, awe, or terror" that our world does not supply.

Next, a reader may be more willing to enter a secondary world and accept what happens there, thus being more open to ideas in the story. Recognizing that the work is fantasy, he willingly suspends disbelief and accepts another world's laws. For example, the main characters are taken to another world and experience anything without straining credibility. When they return to earth, they apply the things they learned. Because the secondary world is a mirror or metaphor for our own, things that happen in that world can be applied to our world. By showing us things in a different way, the other world sheds light on our world and helps us return to it with renewed vision.

Lewis gives advice on how to write about other worlds. First, the secondary world must not be a backdrop for a story that could have been told in another way. The purpose of this world is to create wonder, serve as a metaphor for our world, and catch the reader unaware. It must also be different enough from our world to make it worth going to faerie for, and something must happen once you get there. Finally, the writer must not break the spell and bring the reader back to earth. (*Letters* 468).

> "Narnia? What's that?" said Lucy. "This is the land of Narnia," said the Faun, "where we are now; all that lies between the lamp-post and the great castle of Cair Paravel on the Eastern Sea."
> *The Lion*

A key quality of this other world is believability. Tolkien insists that the secondary world should be presented as true, with an inner consistency of reality, internal logic, and laws that make things explainable. The moment the reader disbelieves, then the spell is broken, and the art fails. Lewis, on the other hand, says the writer needs to put only enough science in the story to create a "willing suspension of disbelief." Details that encourage believability include geography, maps, history, literature, and invented names.

Although the Chronicles are modelled after fairy tales rather than science fiction, Lewis does provide details about the creation of Narnia, its history, and geography. He also includes other characteristics of fairy tales.

The Creation of Narnia

According to Lewis's timeline for Narnia, Narnia was created in 1900 A.D. Why did Lewis call his country "Narnia"? Lewis possibly got the name from Latin literature, where there are at least seven references to "Narnia." Although the children enter a world of Nothingness, Narnia is still a potential, "waiting" to be born, and they feel solid earth beneath them. Aslan creates it by singing, "the most beautiful noise Digory had ever heard." Other voices blend in harmony with it, but in "higher, cold, tingling, silvery voices" that become stars, constellations, and planets bursting into sight in the sky. Narnia has its own constellations (the Ship, Hammer, and Leopard), stars (Spear-head, the North star), and planets (Tarva, and Alambil). Narnia's moon is larger than our's.

Next, as the sky becomes lighter, Digory can see the many colors of a "fresh, hot and vivid earth"; then a young sun arises, laughing with joy. A soft, rippling music produces first grass, then trees. By now, Polly notices a connection between the notes Aslan is singing and the things he is creating. For example, a series of deep, prolonged notes produces dark fir trees; light, rapid notes produce primroses. But a wild, invigorating tune produces humps in the ground from which a joyous menagerie of animals emerges: moles, dogs, stags, frogs, panthers, leopards, showers of birds, butterflies, bees, and elephants. It becomes clear that Aslan's creations are things he imagines, and the song comes from these ideas in his mind. It is a song so special that it makes you hot and flushed, wanting to jump and shout.

This idea of God creating the universe through singing it into being is found also in Tolkien's *Silmarillion* in which Eru creates the Ainor, or Holy Ones, as offspring of his thought and propounds to them musical themes.

Harmoniously, they sing before him a Great Music, whereas evil and proud beings desire to sing their own music that results in discord. Both Lewis and Tolkien seem to be drawing on a medieval concept that uses music as a metaphor for the harmony of the universe. The ancients believed that the planets, for example, were aligned in such exact mathematical relationships that they gave off a special music—the Music of the Spheres. In this scheme, the universe is represented as a musical instrument that includes all creation, from angels to stones. The hand of God stretches out to tune it.

After singing Narnia into being, Aslan speaks: "Narnia, Narnia, Narnia, awake. Love. Think. Speak. Be walking trees. Be talking beasts. Be divine waters."

Lewis draws on another rich metaphor of the Middle Ages that other writers, such as Tolkien and Madeleine L'Engle, have also used in their works. The Great Dance, like the Music of the Spheres, was a metaphor for the perfect harmony, joy, order, and unity of the universe, in which every person, animal, planet, and microorganism played its part in a precisely patterned rhythm. Just as creation and the created universe was an act of music and in a state of music, it also was believed to be in a perpetual Dance. Ramandu, for example, says that when he has been rejuvenated, he will once again rise and tread the measures of this Great Dance.

The Great Snow Dance, described in *The Silver Chair*, is especially unique. On the first moonlit night when snow is on the ground, a ring of dwarfs dressed in fine clothes throw snowballs in perfect time to the sound of wild music. If everyone is in the right place, no one gets hit.

Battle With Evil

After Aslan creates Narnia, he notices that even though this land is barely five hours old, "an evil has already entered it" (a "Neevil," as the creatures call it). Some people argue that fairy tales frighten children, especially if they vividly portray battles and wicked characters. Narnia certainly contains a diversity of evil—"ogres with monstrous teeth, and wolves and bull-headed men; spirits of evil trees and poisonous plants"; cruels, hags, incubuses, wraiths, horrors, efreets, sprites, orknies, wooses, ettins, ghouls, boggles, minotaurs, spectres, people of the toadstools, and other creatures whom Lewis says he won't describe because if he did "the grown-ups would probably not let you read this book."

Lewis was concerned that the Dark Island was too frightening and that he wasn't sure what would frighten readers (*Letters to Children* 33-4). However, he was opposed to the idea that we must protect a child from the knowledge that he is "born into a world of death, violence, wounds adventure, heroism and cowardice, good and evil." This type of protection would encourage escapism. Because the child will undoubtedly meet cruel and horrifying enemies, he should also hear of and admire brave knights, heroic courage, comforters and protectors. So let there be "wicked kings and beheadings, battles and dungeons, giants and dragons, and let villains be soundly killed at the end of the book" (*On Stories* 39-40).

Although good beings are important, depicting hell and evil helps us visualize their reality. The predominant plot of religious fantasy is the war between good and evil. By portraying evil, fantasy exposes readers to the inevitability of sin and death. Evil is usually depicted as not originally bad but a perversion, mockery, or absence of good. It is often associated with blackness and inability to create, cooperate, and trust. The Narnia tales contrast courtesy, courage, community, selflessness, and respect for animals and nature with cowardice, isolation, selfishness, and abuse of animals and nature.

Evil is also portrayed as deceptive and difficult to discern because it appears in many disguises. Both the White Witch and the Queen of Underland are beautiful, thus illustrating the allure and deceptiveness of temptation.

Jadis

According to Lewis, Jadis, the White Witch, is the same evil person found in fairy tales that we are born knowing. He compares her to Circe, who, in *The Odyssey*, tempted men with magical food and turned them into animals. She is one-half giant and one-half Jinn. The Jinn are descended from Lilith who, according to Jewish mythology, was Adam's first wife but refused to obey him and became Satan's dam. She is "bad all through"; in fact, Lewis says she is very much "fallen" (*Letters to Children* 93).

Yet Jadis is exceedingly beautiful, with a look of such fierce, wild pride that she seems "ten times more alive than most people in London." Often compared to Hans Christian Andersen's Snow Queen, she is seven feet tall and dressed all in white fur, with a gold wand and crown. Her face is "white like snow or paper or icing sugar, except for her very red mouth. It was a beautiful face in other respects, but proud and cold and stern." She is also physically powerful and can even hear men's thoughts.

Jadis's history begins as she battles against her sister, who refuses to yield her the throne of Charn. In revenge, Jadis speaks the "Deplorable Word" that destroys all living things when spoken. She had learned this word in a "secret place" and paid a "terrible price" for it. With that word she casts all of Charn and its inhabitants into a frozen enchantment. Under one of her spells, the Witch promises to sleep among them like a statue until someone strikes a bell to awaken her.

Digory and Polly, of course, discover her asleep in the courtroom. On a four-foot high square pillar is a golden arch from which hangs a golden bell. Beside it lies a golden hammer inscribed on its side with the following words: "Make your choice, adventurous Stranger; Strike the bell and bide the danger, Or wonder, till it drives you mad, What would have followed if you had."

Wild with curiosity—"I wonder . . . I wonder . . . I wonder"—Digory finally strikes the bell. At first it gives off a sweet sound, which, instead of dying away, grows unbearably loud until it awakens the Witch. Later, Digory admits to Aslan that he simply wanted to know what would happen if he struck the bell; he wasn't really enchanted by the letters. The children escape to the Wood between the Worlds by touching their yellow rings. But Jadis, first grabbing Polly's hair and then Digory's ears, stays with them until they are back in London.

Later, the Witch enters Narnia by Digory grabbing hold of her ankle. Rebelling against another new world, she hurls the iron bar from the lamp-post in England at Aslan's forehead. But it comes to life where it falls, growing up as a young lamp-post. Afterwards, this lamp shines day and night in the Narnian forest, and the area where it stands is called Lantern Waste.

After the Witch flees north, the Tree of Protection keeps her from Narnia for 897 years. Then Jadis returns to rule Narnia as Queen for 100 years. As we see in *The Lion, the Witch and the Wardrobe,* her reign is accompanied by continuous winter, and Christmas never comes.

But in this story, she meets her end. Although she can turn other people to stone with a flick of her wand, she is weaker than Aslan: "Turn him into stone? If she can stand on her two feet and look him in the face it'll be the most she can do." When she challenges his promise to die for Edmund, one mighty roar from Aslan sends her running. She believes she is victorious in killing Aslan on the Stone Table. But she is ignorant of the Deeper Magic that invalidates all her claims to the victim and reverses Death itself. With a roar that shakes all of Narnia, Aslan flings himself into battle against Jadis. With an expression of "terror and amazement," she is killed.

Green Witch

Jadis is not to be confused with the Green Witch in *The Silver Chair*, ruler of the Shallow-Lands, though they are of the same lineage. Like Jadis, the Green Witch is deceptively beautiful: she wears "a long fluttering dress of dazzling green" and laughs in the "richest, most musical laugh you can imagine." But her true nature is revealed when she changes into a serpent, traditionally the symbol of Satan and evil.

Probably the most vivid example of the wiles of the witches is the enchantment of Jill, Eustace, and Puddleglum in *The Silver Chair*. The Green Witch flings a green powder into the air and strums a mandolin, both of which confuse their minds, making thinking difficult. Through her enchantment, she begins to convince them that their world is but a dream and her lamp the real sun: "You can put nothing into your make-believe without copying it from the real world, this world of mine, which is the only world." Lewis writes:

> Do you think I am trying to weave a spell? Perhaps I am;
> but remember your fairy tales. Spells are used for breaking
> enchantments as well as for inducing them. And you and I have
> need of the strongest spell that can be found to wake us from the

evil enchantment of worldliness which has been laid upon us for nearly a hundred years (*Weight* 5).

Magic

According to Narnian history, the Emperor-Over-Sea sent a Deep Magic into the world from the "Dawn of Time." This Magic permits the Witch to kill every traitor, and unless she has blood, Narnia will perish in water and fire. But further back in time is a Deeper Magic about which the Witch knows nothing. This Law states that when a willing victim who has committed no treachery is killed in the traitor's stead, the Stone Table will crack, and Death will start working backwards.

A theme in *The Magician's Nephew* is the bad use of magic to control other people. Both Jadis and Uncle Andrew claim that their's is a "high and lonely destiny." Uncle Andrew, who only dabbles in magic, seeks to use the children and to exploit his discoveries in other worlds. Digory calls him "a wicked, cruel magician like the ones in the stories." Jadis, like other tyrants, does not care for joy, justice, or mercy. She is not interested in things or people; rather, people exist only to do her will, and she is "terribly practical." She paid a "terrible price" for her knowledge and power.

In "On Fairy Stories," Tolkien distinguishes between two kinds of magic: "magia" (good) and "goeteia" (bad); however, either can become good or bad depending on the "motive or purpose or use." For example, a bad motive is to dominate the free wills of others or deceive. Magia, on the other hand, is used for "specific beneficent purposes." Magic is an inherent power than men cannot possess, obtain, or achieve by spells.

In religious fantasy, magic comes from God, and a central theme of the book is usually the characters' relationship to Him. When Aslan appears to Lucy and Susan after his death on the Stone Table, he says, "It is more magic." The Supreme Being, the source of good magic, gives his followers power that they often evoke through the magic aid of prayer. For example, the children pray and do things in Aslan's name. Lucy is given a magic cordial that is used to heal. In contrast, evil creatures selfishly misuse magic by seeking to control others. Thus the witches seek to dominate and control and can make things look like what they are not. Even the Magician's Magic Book, which contains the most wonderful story, can be misused. It tempts Lucy to say a spell to make herself beautiful, and she succumbs to learning what others think of her.

> "I didn't believe in Magic till today. I see now it's real. Well if it is, I suppose all the old fairy tales are more or less true."
> Digory, *The Magician's Nephew*

An essential nature of fairy story, then, is magic, and in the case of religious fantasy, the source of magic is usually the supernatural. Lewis defines magic as "objective efficacy which cannot be further analysed" (*Letters to Malcolm* 103). It is not what he calls "paltry and pathetic techniques" used to control nature. Instead, he gives the example of sentences in fairy tales: "This is a magic cave and those who enter it will renew their youth." The magical element in Christianity is "that the heavenly realm, certainly no less than the natural universe and perhaps very much more, is a realm of objective facts" (104).

Instead of "magic," Tolkien prefers the term "Enchantment," the creation of a secondary world into which both designer and spectator can enter. The idea of a parallel world reached only by magic is a favorite device in fantasy. It is through magic—a magic wardrobe, magic horn, a magic picture, and magic rings—that the children of our world enter Narnia: "How did you get there?" said Jill. . . "The only way you can—by Magic," says Eustace almost in a whisper.

Narnia is described as "really another world—another Nature." Professor Kirke suggests that there are probably other worlds right "around the corner." But the "chinks" or "chasms" that connect these worlds are growing rarer. In *The Magician's Nephew*, Uncle Andrew describes Narnia as one of these secret countries that is real—"a really other world—another Nature—another universe," a place you will never reach except by Magic.

Entering and Exiting Narnia

The children enter Narnia through curiosity, such as exploring the house in *The Magician's Nephew,* or the wardrobe, or when things are "at their worst." Professor Kirke explains that the children can never get into Narnia a second time by the same route. In fact, they can't try to get there at all. Instead, Aslan calls them in his own way and time, and it happens when they aren't expecting it. The children are usually summoned to Narnia when someone "in a pinch" needs them, although they are assured that there are many, many years of peace in Narnia. But Aslan says that the main reason they are brought to Narnia is "that by knowing me here for a little, you may know me better there." The only way to Aslan's country from all worlds is across a river bridged by Aslan himself.

In *The Magician's Nephew*, Digory and Polly enter by means of yellow rings that only need to be touched. They were made from dust in a box from the lost city of

Atlantis that Uncle Andrew obtained from his godmother. Because the material of the rings is from another world that existed when ours was just beginning, it draws one back into the place where it came from. So Digory and Polly come up through a pool into the Wood Between the Worlds.

The green rings, on the other hand, transport them out of the Wood and into a new world. The experience of leaving is brief but doesn't happen too quickly for Digory to note bright lights—the stars and even Jupiter's moons—moving around him. More remarkable, as he gets closer to England, he can even see through the walls of houses, and objects that were at first shadowy come sharply into focus. At the end of their adventures in this book, the children simply have to look at Aslan's face, and they are back in England for good.

Narnia is reached in a different way made famous in *The Lion, the Witch and the Wardrobe.* Digory takes a special apple from a Narnian tree and plants the core in his back yard. Although a storm ruins the tree that subsequently grows, he makes a magic wardrobe out of the salvaged wood. Then, many years later, after Digory has become old Professor Kirke, Lucy Pevensie climbs into the wardrobe and steps behind the coats and mothballs into Lantern Waste.

Yet when the other three children try to confirm her wild tale of a secret country, all they find is hard wood at the back of the wardrobe. So, again, one can't try to get into Narnia. To return to England from Narnia even after 15 Narnian years have passed, all the children have to do is to walk back through the coats and into the wardrobe. This wardrobe is reminiscent of the Stable in *The Last Battle,* whose inside is bigger than its outside and that leads the Narnians into another world.

The children are not called to Narnia again until one day, sitting dejectedly at the train station waiting to return to school, they feel themselves "pulled" and then suddenly scratched with branches. Caspian has blown Susan's magic horn, which always brings help when used. The children's return to England is more spectacular. Like the special Door that appears in *The Last Battle*, Aslan sets up two wooden stakes three feet apart, with a third binding them together at the top, thus creating a doorway "from nowhere into nowhere." Through this doorway, the Telmarines pass back into the South Seas of our world. Then the children sorrowfully pass through "layers" and see three curious things: first, a cave opening to a Pacific Island; next, a glade in Narnia; and, finally, the gray platform of the country station, just as it was when they left England.

The Voyage of the "Dawn Treader" begins in still a different way. On Eustace Scrubb's bedroom wall is a lovely picture of a sailing ship on the sea. But the more Lucy stares at it, the more real and alive the scene becomes. In fact, the waves start to roll up and down, and the air smells wild and briny. Lucy, Edmund and Eustace are even slapped in the face with salt water. As the incorrigible Eustace attempts to smash the picture, he finds himself standing on the frame, then swept into the sea. At the end of their long adventure, Lucy and Edmund are told that they are too old to return to Narnia again. Then Aslan returns all three of them to Cambridge by ripping the blue sky like a curtain and letting them through.

That same year, Eustace and his schoolmate, Jill Pole, despairing of their dreary life at a school called Experiment House, really *try* to get into Narnia. Eustace tells Jill he has been to the kind of place you read about in fairy tales, and the only way you can get there is by

Magic. Jill questions whether using black magic, such as charms and spells, might work. But Eustace, calling such methods "rot," replies that they can't make Aslan do things. Instead, "we can only ask him."

As they rush away from the noise of their approaching schoolmates, they throw open a usually locked door in a high stone wall. But instead of seeing a heathery moor, they find the cool bright air and vibrant forest of Aslan's country. At the end of their mission to rescue Rilian, they triumphantly return to Experiment House—this time with Aslan—who simply leads them through the woods to the school.

Of course, in the final trip to Narnia, every one of the "friends of Narnia" on earth is called to Narnia by means of an actual train accident that instantly kills them all. Jill and Eustace, however, immediately find themselves with Tirian when he needs them the most. We don't know what happened right away to the others, but we do know they ended up in Aslan's country—this time, to stay.

History

After Lewis wrote the seven stories, he drew up an outline of Narnia's history. A historical time-chart of Narnia, based on Lewis's outline and the information found in the stories themselves, is shown on the next page. There are 2555 Narnian years between its creation and destruction, corresponding to 52 earth years. During the history of Narnia, there was an "Old Narnia" and a "New Narnia."

The former consisted of years of peace and joy, when every day and week was better than the last. Narnia is only "right" when humans rule. There is not always peace in Narnia because it is surrounded by powerful enemies who could always invade it. (It is relatively small—one

Narnian Chronology

Chronology based upon Lewis' outline of Narnian History as far as it is known. *Past Watchful Dragons* by Walter Hooper, *Imagine and the Spirit*, pp. 41-4, and the Narnia books themselves

Book	Earth Time	Narnia Time	Narnian Period	Ruler: Narnia(*) Archenland(^)	Key Events
MN	1900	0		Frank & Helen*	Narnia crested and witch flies north
	1927	200		Frank V* / Col^ (son of Frank V)	Archenland established / Calormen established
	1930 / 1933			Gale* (also emperor of Lone Islands)	Telmar colonized by Calormenes / Telmarenes wicked and made dumb; land lies waste / Olvin of Archenland kills Giant Pire; Mt Pire created / Pirates take over Telmar
		400			
		600			Moonwood the Hare
		800			
HHB / LWW	1940	1000	Long Winter / Golden Age	Jadis, White Witch* / Peter* Lune^ Cor & Aravis^ Ram the Great^ (son of Cor)	Jadis returns to Narnia / Aslan's sacrifice / Peter raids N. giants
		1200			
		1400			
		1600		Queen Swanwhite*	
		1800	Old Narnia		
		2000	New Narnia	(Nain) Caspian I*	Telmarines conquer Narnia
PC VDT SC	1941	2200	Civil War	Caspian IX* / Mirax & Prunaprismia*	
	1942	2400		Caspian X* (2290-2356) / Rilian* (2325-?)	Caspian defeats N. Giants
LB	1949		Final Days	Erlian* Tirian*	Outlaws in Lantern Waste; protective towers built / Destruction of Narnia (2555)

Key to Abbreviations:

MN: *Magician's Nephew*
HHB: *The Horse and His Boy*
LWW: *The Lion, the Witch and the Wardrobe*
PC: *Prince Caspian*
VDT: *Voyage of the Dawn Treader*
SC: *Silver Chair*
LB: *The Last Battle*

quarter the size of the smallest Calormene province). But for the most part, there are years and years of peace and joyful activities—dances, feasts, and great tournaments; hunting parties, treasure-seeking, and midnight dances.

The four Pevensie children rule during the Golden Age. To recollect those happy years is like "looking down from a high hill onto a rich, lovely plain full of woods and waters and cornfields, which spread away and away till it got thin and misty from distance."

Peter is the oldest Pevensie, followed by Susan, Edmund, and Lucy. Because of the air-raids during the war, they are sent from London to stay with Professor Kirke. On their first adventure, Peter is 13 years old, Susan 12, Edmund 10, and Lucy 8. In 1941, they are called back to Narnia to aid Prince Caspian, after which Peter and Susan are told they are too old to return to Narnia. One year later when Lucy and Edmund are sent to Cambridge to stay with their Aunt and Uncle, they join Eustace Scrubb, their cousin, and sail on the "Dawn Treader." Peter at this time is being tutored for an exam by Professor Kirke. Their parents, on the other hand, are in the United States for 16 weeks while Mr. Pevensie lectures, and Susan tags along since she is "poor at schoolwork" anyway.

In 1949, Digory and Polly, now 61 and 62 years old, feel they all are "needed" in Narnia and send Peter and Edmund after the magic rings Digory had buried in London. As the others—Jill, Eustace, Digory, Polly, Lucy, and, by chance, Mr. and Mrs. Pevensie—come to meet them on the train, a train crash kills all of them instantly.

As the timeline for Narnia indicates, there is an obvious and distinct difference between the time frames of Narnia and England: 2555 years of Narnia from beginning to end correspond to just 49 earth years from 1900-1949. Yet two Narnian years pass between 1930 and 1933 and 698

> "Most of us, I suppose, have a secret country but for us it is only an imaginary country. Edmund and Lucy were luckier than other people in that respect. Their secret country was real."
>
> *The Voyage of the "Dawn Treader"*

years between 1933 and 1940. One earth year does not equal one Narnian year. Just what was Lewis up to?

First, it is quite common in stories for two worlds to have different times; even Tirian acknowledges this fact. Professor Kirke explains to the children that if there is a separate world, it would not be unusual for it to have a time of its own "so that however long you stayed there it would never take up any of our time." As a result, each time the children return from Narnia to England, they find no time has passed on earth, no matter how long they have been busy in Narnia.

For example, Digory, Polly, and the whole crew of Cabby, horse, and Witch leave England and witness all the glorious events of Narnia's creation and the establishment of the new kingdom. Then Digory and Polly return right into the middle of the very mess the Witch had created. Lucy emerges breathlessly from the Wardrobe without a second having ticked away; and when all four "Kings and Queens" return after their 15 year reign, they return "the same day and the same hour of the day on which they had all gone into the wardrobe to hide."

A second "muddle about time," which seems to take the children quite a while to get used to, is the fact that Narnian time flows differently from ours. So once you're out of Narnia, you have no idea how Narnian time is

A Guide Through Narnia

going. You can spend 100 years in Narnia and return to our world the same hour you left. Or you could return to Narnia and find 1000 Narnian years or no time had passed: "You never know till you get there." In *Prince Caspian*, the children have only been gone from Narnia one year but find it entirely grown over and so changed they can't recognize it, for it is hundreds of Narnian years later. Yet in *The Voyage of the "Dawn Treader"* when they return after another year in England, only three Narnian years have passed since Caspian's coronation.

Each time the children go to Narnia, they find Narnian time has flowed differently from earth time. Whenever the children become too old, they are not allowed to return to Narnia. Walter Hooper explains that Lewis knew what he was doing here; for he believed that other worlds might have a time with "thicknesses and thinnesses," not a linear time like ours (*Past* 40). Hooper feels this technique has two important effects. Not only do the strange time lapses allow more interesting adventures, but they also teach the children about history itself. Because they do not know what stage of Narnian history they are playing a role in, the children cannot see the meaning of the whole plan; only Aslan does. Aslan "calls all times soon." Lewis believed it was right to make the children grow up in Narnia even though they were children in England because age doesn't matter (*Letters to Children* 34).

Geography

Just as Lewis provides a timeline, he mapped his own rough conception of Narnian topography. From this sketch, Pauline Baynes later drew a more detailed map for Lewis. In addition, by gathering information from the seven Narnia tales, we get a fairly comprehensive idea of the geography of Narnia and the surrounding countries.

Narnia

Narnia itself seems to resemble Lewis's favorite parts of the English and Irish countrysides, with its avenues of beeches, sunny oak glades, deep forests, and orchards of snow-white cherry trees; its windy slopes of gorse bushes, acres of blue flowers, wild valleys, and heathery mountains and ridges; its roaring waterfalls, winding rivers, plashy glens, mossy rocks and caverns.

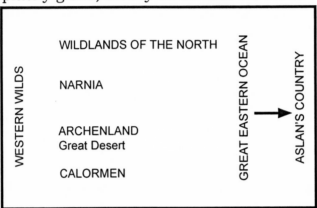

The low hills to the *north* and the moorlands lead to the wild and desolate land of the giant stronghold, described predominantly in *The Silver Chair*. This Northern land of barren, rocky plains, frigid mountains, and stony boulders and ruins has a bleak, windy, snowy climate unlike the rich and dewy atmosphere of Narnia.

The Great Sea lying to the *east* of Narnia contains all the islands visited in *The Voyage of the "Dawn Treader"*: Galma, Terebinthia, the Seven Islands, the Lone Islands, the Dragon, Deathwater, Darkness, and World's End Islands. Beyond this is Aslan's country and the End of the World. In *The Voyage of the "Dawn Treader"*, the topography of Narnia and these countries is described as being like a great, round but flat table with the waters of all the oceans pouring endlessly over the edge.

To the *west* of Narnia is the Western Wild, where one can see high, snow-crowned mountains and glaciers, and verdant valleys with streams tumbling down from the mountains, sparkling like blue jewelry. Here, the Great Waterfall crashes down to create the Caldron Pool; then the River of Narnia winds across the land to the Sea. This is where the beginning and ending of Narnia takes place. The Lantern Waste is the area where the children enter Narnia in *The Lion* and where the lamp-post springs up. Also to the west of Narnia is Telmar.

South of Narnia is another ridge of mountains across which lie two countries: Archenland, connected to Narnia by a pass, and Calormen, across a sandy desert.

Telmar

The story of the "New Narnia" begins with the story of Telmar. Telmar, an island beyond the Western Mountains of Narnia, is first colonized by the Calormenes in the year 300 (Narnian time). When these Calormenes behave wickedly, Aslan turns them into Dumb Beasts, and the country is laid waste. Then 160 years later, some pirates in our world are driven by storm onto an island in the South Seas. They kill the natives and take native women as their wives. One day they become drunk and quarrel. Six flee with the women to the center of the island, then climb up a mountain into a cave. This cave is a "chink" or "chasm" between worlds, and they fall through to the uninhabited land of Telmar.

Their descendants become fierce and proud. In the Narnian year 1998, there is a famine, and Caspian I of Telmar leads an invasion of Narnia and becomes king. But the Telmarines begin to change Narnia, for they silence the beasts, trees and fountains; kill and drive away the dwarfs and fauns, and try to erase all memory of them. Because they fear the Sea, they let woods grow up around Cair Paravel and the coast to separate them from the water. Then, because they hate the trees, they invent a story that these Black Woods are full of ghosts. So by the time of Prince Caspian, both the Telmarines and Old Narnians have forgotten the truth about Old Narnia—it is all "just stories." Caspian admits that he has often wondered if Aslan is real and if there actually were any Talking Beasts and dwarfs.

As we know from the story of *Prince Caspian*, Narnia is restored to the old order. At the end of the book, Aslan allows those who wish to go back to the South Sea island—a land of good wells, fresh water, fruitful soil, timber, and fish—through a special doorway. That chasm between the two worlds is then closed forever.

Archenland

Archenland is a smaller country south of Narnia separated from it by mountains. It is a "delightful" and "glorious" country of fresh green hills, "pine-clad slopes, frowning cliffs, narrow gorges, and blue peaks." In 180, Col, the youngest son of Frank and Helen, led followers to Archenland and became their first king. In 204, outlaws from Archenland fled south across the desert, founding Calormen.

Calormen

Far to the south of Narnia, below Archenland and across the mountains and a great desert, lies Calormen. As Lewis describes the Calormenes and their capital city, they are reminiscent of the Turks or Arabians. Supposedly, Lewis disliked *The Arabian Nights* and perhaps used that culture as a basis for his invention of the evil enemies of Narnia. Many believe that Lewis negatively portrays Middle-Eastern stereotypes.

Calormen is created in Narnian year 204, when outlaws from Archenland flee south across the desert and set up the kingdom. A Calormene visitor is readily recognized by his spiked helmet projecting from a silken turban, a chain mail shirt, curved scimitar, and crimson dyed beard. Typical Calormenes are "grave," "mysterious," "wise," "cruel," and "ancient," wearing orange turbans, flowing robes and shoes turned up at the toe. Seeming to lack imagination and creativity, the Calormenes write poetry consisting only of maxims and apothegms—about topics other than love and war—and they must be taught to tell stories.

Tashbaan is the Calormene capital, located on an island between two rivers. Buildings rise on either side of the streets that zigzag up the hill and completely cover the island. In between are masses of orange and lemon trees, roof gardens, balconies, archways, battlements, spires, and pinnacles. If you look closely, though, you can see crowded narrow streets full of rude, bumping people and sniff the pervasive smell of garlic, onions, refuse, and unwashed bodies.

The Calormenes adhere rigidly to a strict hierarchy. Although they care nothing for Aslan, they have a deity, Tash—a hideous, birdlike creature with a vulture's or eagle's head and four arms. The ruler is called the Tisroc, under whom are Tarkaans (lords) and Tarkheenas (ladies), such as Aravis or Lasaraleen in the story of *The Horse and His Boy*. Lasaraleen's lifestyle is much like that of a Turkish princess, as she rides proudly atop a platform carried by servants and shielded by lavish curtains.

The Wood Between the Worlds

Besides Narnia and its surrounding countries, there are other worlds described in the books. For example, when Digory is sent to test the magic rings, he has the sensation of coming up into a new world, only to discover that he has entered not a new world, but an "in-between" place from which he can get into other worlds. It contains dozens of pools with a different world at the bottom of each of them. These places will not be named until people live there. Although it is a dreamy, sleepy place where nothing seems to happen, it is alive—warm and rich as a plum cake. The leafy trees grow so close together that they allow only a "green" daylight to seep in, and he can almost hear them growing. Digory feels as though he has always been there. But when the children leave the Wood, they enter a world of Nothing.

Charn

The essence of evil worlds is always a perversion of the good. Entering the cloud of vague, whirling shapes through one of the pools in the Wood Between the Worlds, Digory and Polly find themselves in Charn. Once a great city, "city of the King of kings," "wonder of all worlds," it is now a dying world. Once bustling with slaves, chariots, and ritual drums and sacrifices in the temple, it is now a cold, dead, empty silence devoid of any life. Only temples, towers, palaces, pyramids, and bridges remain. Courtyard after courtyard stands in ruin. The sun is older than ours, giving off a dull, steady, red light in a dark sky, and a stale wind blows. Where once a river flowed that was turned to blood, there is only a ditch. Then, at the very end of *The Magician's Nephew*, the little pool that once led to Charn becomes a dry hollow, signaling the end of its existence and giving a subtle warning to the race of Adam and Eve.

Underland and Bism

In *The Silver Chair*, we learn that Narnia's world has several layers. The Green Witch's world of Underland lies just beneath the ruins of an ancient Northern city and is a perversion of the real world. The children must descend through numerous caverns and suffocating tunnels, each cave lower than the last. There is no wind or birds but only a greenish light, batlike animals, and a city full of docile, miserable Earthmen. Like the River Styx in mythology, a river glides lazily to the Witch's castle.

But the Green Witch's world is sandwiched in between Narnia and another, deeper, wonderful realm. For beneath her false "Shallow-Lands" is Bism. This is the "Really Deep Land," 1000 fathoms beneath the Queen's realm. Bism is the real home of the gnomish Earthmen, to whom living on the Upper World sounds horrible: "You can't really like it—crawling about like flies on the top of the world!" Through a chasm in the earth (from which seeps a strong heat and a rich, sharp, exciting smell) the children can see brilliant fields and groves of hot, bright blues, reds, greens, and whites. The gems there, they learn, are alive. Through all this runs a river of fire inhabited by salamanders.

Lewis is drawing on the ancient tradition that subterranean fire—one of the four elements—was inhabited by gnomes and salamanders. But Bism also seems to represent a far deeper reality that Rilian reluctantly decides not to explore. The gnomes plunge headlong into it, just as Robin, in Lewis's story "The Man Born Blind," dives into the light and warmth symbolic of the beauty Lewis says we long to bathe in.

> "Tirian ... knew that he was looking at one of the great heroes of Narnia, Reepicheep the Mouse, who had ... sailed to the World's end."
> *The Last Battle*

Government

In addition to a well-defined geography, Narnia has a government and hierarchy. It is significant that only a human can serve as King or Queen. Mr. Beaver knows that "When Adam's flesh and Adam's bone Sits at Cair Paravel in throne, The evil time will be over and done." Frank, a simple cabby, feels he is not fit to be a King: "I ain't no sort of chap for a job like that. I never 'ad much eddycation, you see." Yet his voice grows steadily richer, and by the time of his coronation, he has a brand new expression of courage and kindness on his face, without an ounce of quarrelsomeness, sharpness, or cunning. The hero's transformation to the status of king or queen reflects a spiritual change as well.

Lewis seems to be clearly affirming that if we are Christians, we will one day become kings and queens. All of us have this potential. In "The Weight of Glory," he writes:

> It is a serious thing to live in a society of possible gods and goddesses, to remember that the dullest and most uninteresting person you talk to may one day be a creature which, if you saw it now, you would be strongly tempted to worship, or else a horror and corruption such as you now meet, if at all, only in a nightmare. . . . There are no ordinary people. (15)

The Kings and Queens of Narnia rule from a castle on the eastern sea-coast named Cair Paravel (which means an "inferior court," implying its administration is still subordinate to the Emperor-Over-Sea). Life there is reminiscent of the medieval Arthurian setting of coronations, feasts, falconry, rich clothing and courtly language. As in medieval courts, old epics are told aloud; for example, the children hear the story of *The Horse and His Boy* retold many years later. Battle clothes are bright tunics, steel or silver caps covered with jewels and with winged sides, and straight swords; their banner depicts a red Lion.

Yet the subjects of this monarchy retain their freedom; in fact, there is no slavery at all in Narnia—not even marriage against one's will. Aslan instructs King Frank, first Narnian King, that a good King rules kindly and fairly, with no favorites, and is to be first in the charge and last in retreat from enemies.

The following are the rulers of Narnia and Archenland that Lewis mentions:

- Frank and Helen
- Frank V
- Col of Archenland
- Gale
- Olvin
- Peter, Edmund, Susan, Lucy
- Lune of Archenland
- Cor and Aravis of Archenland
- Ram of Archenland
- Swanwhite
- Caspian I
- Capian VIII
- Caspian IX
- Nain of Archenland
- Caspian X & Daughter of Ramandu

- Rilian
- Erlian
- Tirian

During the creation of Narnia, Aslan chooses two of each animal by touching their noses with his. These become Talking Beasts, which are put in charge of the Dumb Beasts. The hierarchy of Narnia is as follows:

- The Emperor-Over-Sea and his son Aslan Peter (High King)
- Kings and Queens
- Minor nobility
- Talking Beasts and longaevi ("long-livers," creatures such as nymphs, satyrs and centaurs.)
- Dumb Beasts

Talking Animals and Other Creatures

Tolkien believed that fairy tales fulfill our desires, such as communicating with other living beings. There are nine classes of Narnian creatures:

- Waking Trees
- Visible Naiads
- Fauns
- Satyrs
- Dwarfs
- Giants
- Gods
- Centaurs
- Talking Beasts

Lewis believed that the presence of beings other than humans, who behave humanly—"giants and dwarfs and

Talking Beasts"—is a central element in all fairy tales. There are several reasons for this. First, the writer can give these animal characters a child's carefree life with no domestic or other responsibilities. Yet they are like adults because they can do what and go where they wish. In addition, animals are frequently used in fantasy as aids and comforters. Lewis considers it important to have such protectors side by side with terrible creatures (*On Stories* 40). Animals can also portray personality types most succinctly to a wide audience. Lewis gives the example of Mr. Badger in *The Wind in the Willows*. Any child who has met Mr. Badger has "a knowledge of humanity and of English social history which it could not get in any other way" (*On Stories* 36). Where do we see courage more clearly than in the swashbuckling Reepicheep, a two-foot mouse, proudly and fearlessly defending and jabbing with his small sword? Mrs. Beaver is a particularly memorable stereotype of the practical housewife who takes time to pack clean hankies, ham, tea, and sugar—"I suppose the sewing machine's too heavy to bring?"

Lewis certainly has a convincing way of combining their humanness with their innate animal characteristics—the "cawing, cooing, crowing, braying, neighing, baying, barking, lowing, bleating, and trumpeting"; the "wagging tails, and barking, and loose slobbery mouths and noses of dogs thrust into your hand." The animals act according to their nature and skills. For example, each animal has a role to play in the battle with the witch by doing what it is best at. Glimfeather the owl is wise. Bree the horse snobbishly worries about his looks, considers humans "funny little creatures," and speaks to the mare, Hwin, instead of her mistress, Aravis. He patronizes Shasta, and, worst of all, doubts that Aslan is a real lion. But how "horsey" he is, too, doing that which he likes best and is afraid of losing in Narnia: rubbing his back on the turf and waving his legs in the air.

When a writer uses animals in fantasy, he creates a world we wish were true: an Eden where lion and lamb can lie down together and where animals talk. Animals satisfy our desire to communicate with animals. But they can also help us understand deeper meanings. For example, when Eustace turns into a dragon in *The Voyage of the "Dawn Treader,"* we can ultimately see his peeling away layers of scales as an image of salvation. As seen in *The Last Battle*, Talking Beasts must choose between right and wrong. The way animals are treated also reflects the conditions of a person or society.

Reepicheep

Narnian life illustrates the difference in values. Where else but in Narnia could a mouse be respected as the most valiant of all the beasts? Reepicheep is perhaps based on Lewis's love for mice. Although mice were not originally Talking Beasts, Aslan gave them this honor because they nibbled away at the cords that held him to the Stone Table after his sacrificial death.

The Chief Mouse is Reepicheep, most valiant of all the Talking Beasts of Narnia, who won undying glory in the second Battle of Beruna. Standing on his hind legs, he is about two-feet tall. Passing under one ear, over the other, and around his head is a thin band of gold with a crimson feather stuck in it. His sword is almost as long as his tail, yet he has perfect balance. Always using courtly manners, he twirls his whiskers like a long moustache.

The mouse's small size deceptively hides his abundant, often impulsive courage. In *Prince Caspian*, for example, when he graciously offers his men's services in Caspian's army, Caspian tries hard not to laugh. Naturally, it is he who first offers to step through Aslan's door to the island of the Telmarines. In *The Voyage of the "Dawn Treader,"* we get an even better look at Reepicheep. Voluntarily serving as sentry over the water, he indignantly jabs for his honor at Eustace, who mockingly swirls him through the air by the tail. He is first to volunteer to fight single-handedly against dragons. The mouse even plays chess daringly by sending his knight into the combined danger of queen and castle, because "his mind was full of forlorn hopes, death or glory charges, and last stands."

It is Reepicheep who wants to press on to the Dark Island for the greatest of adventures and to keep their honor. He is first to eat at Aslan's Table and refuses to leave it. Not only is it a great adventure, but "no danger seems to me so great as that of knowing when I get back to Narnia that I left a mystery behind me through fear." Then he is the first to believe in the foods and the truthfulness of Ramandu's daughter: "I will drink to the lady," he cries, as he valiantly raises his cup in the air.

His quest to reach the World's End has an Arthurian flavor: "The spell of it has been on me all my life," he says. In his letters to children, Lewis says Reepicheep is like anyone who devotes his or her life to seeking Heaven (*Letters to Children* 45). Quivering with excitement at the adventure's end, Reepicheep is determined to go on. He will sail east in the "Dawn Treader." If the boat fails, he will paddle east in his coracle. And if that sinks, "I shall swim east with my four paws." As he throws his sword into the sea, it stands up with its hilt above the surface like Arthur's Excalibur, a sign of valor. Indeed, he does reach Aslan's country, for who else but Reepicheep later welcomes the children at the golden gates of Aslan's garden. He is thus only character who does not die.

Reepicheep seems not only immune from fear and loss of dignity but also from greed and envy. Surprisingly, he comforts Eustace when he is a dragon, telling him stories of greater people who have fallen, and Eustace never forgets it. He also keeps out of the quarrel over the gold on Deathwater Island.

Reepicheep's courage and dignity are so extraordinary, however, that Aslan expresses concern that he may be overcome by vanity. In *Prince Caspian*, the mouse loses his tail and thus his balance in battle; so he requests a new tail, because "a tail is the honour and glory of a Mouse." When Aslan questions whether he does not think too much about his honour, Reepicheep replies that because mice are so small, "if we did not guard our dignity, some (who weigh worth by inches) would allow themselves very unsuitable pleasantries at our expense." Aslan grants him his wish, not because of his dignity, but because of the love and kindness of his people.

Puddleglum

Puddleglum the Marshwiggle is perhaps Lewis's most unique creation. He has a long thin face, sunken cheeks, and a tightly-shut mouth. Topped by a high, flat-brimmed hat pointed like a steeple, his grayish green "hair" hangs over his ears and has round locks that look "like tiny reeds." His solemn expression and "muddy complexion" show that he has a "very serious view of life." He has very long legs and arms, and webbed hands and feet, like a frog. Like all Marshwiggles, who enjoy their privacy, he lives in a wigwam in the reedy marshes.

Lewis, according to Green and Hooper, based the character of Puddleglum on his gardener Fred Paxford, who was similarly unusual and given to "gloomy prognostications": "an inwardly optimistic, outwardly pessimistic, dear, frustrating, shrewd country man of immense integrity" (123). Indeed, poor Puddleglum always expects the worst of every possible situation: "Very likely, what with enemies, and mountains, and rivers to cross, and losing our way, and next to nothing to eat, and sore feet, we'll hardly notice the weather."

> "Puddleglum's my name. But it doesn't matter if you forget it. I can always tell you again."
> *The Silver Chair*

Yet isn't he the perfect guide for Eustace and Jill on their mission to save Rilian? His cold-blooded clear-sightedness and reliability are invaluable in the frozen lands of the North. His pessimism keeps him from too readily succumbing to giants or witches, and he remembers Aslan's rules when the children fail. During the Witch's enchantment, for example, he stout-heartedly stamps out the fire with his webbed foot and solidly denounces her world: "I'm on Aslan's side even if there isn't any Aslan to lead it. I'm going to live as like a Narnian as I can even if there isn't any Narnia."

Style

Lewis uses humor and other techniques to tell his stories, many of which are typical of the fairy tale form.

Humor

Reepicheep and Puddleglum are examples of the touches of humor throughout the Chronicles. Lewis uses both subtle and direct humor. For example, the Parliament of Owls in *The Silver Chair* is a play on Chaucer's *Parliament of Fowls*. Shasta and Aravis are so used to quarreling and making up that they get married so they can do it conveniently. The Head of Experiment House behaves like a lunatic when Aslan comes to Jill's and Eustace's despicable school. After an inquiry, the Head is made an Inspector "to interfere with other Heads." But when she fails at that job, she gets into Parliament, "where she lived happily ever after."

Various characters are satires of common personality types and sometimes receive humorous and ridiculous "rewards" for their actions. For example, Uncle Andrew, the proud and foolish dabbler in magic, is always out for his own skin. Apparently he has mismanaged all of his sister's money. If his vanity isn't bad enough, he greedily plots to commercialize Narnia by burying coins or valuables and letting them spring up into trees. With his mop of hair, he is mistaken for a tree. What a fitting punishment when the animals plant him—fortunately, right-side up—and then the elephant appropriately hoses him. Each animal kindly feeds him with nuts, worms, and globs of honey (plus bees). Aslan, calling him simply an "old sinner" who cannot hear his voice, puts him to sleep.

In *The Horse and His Boy*, Rabadash receives a similar judgment. Rabadash believes Narnia has changed due to alteration of the stars. He impetuously attacks Archenland for his own private purpose of getting back at Susan and fulfilling his premature desire for the throne. His reward is to be suspended from the castle wall in battle, hooked by his own chain-shirt to a peg in the wall. Still, he indignantly threatens vengeance on Lune's forces for this undignified insult. Although Aslan warns him to cast aside his pride and anger, he bombards them with curses until his nemesis: his ears become pointed and covered with gray hair; his face grows long and thick. Then he stands up on all fours until he is unmistakably a donkey. Yet Aslan's justice is tempered with mercy, for as long as Rabadash does not stray from Tash's temple, he will remain a human.

In *The Voyage of the "Dawn Treader,"* Gumpas is the bilious governor of the Lone Islands and the stereotype of the "progressive" politician. (How fitting that "gump" means dolt or numbskull). He sticks mechanically to his appointment schedule, forms, rules and regulations, ledgers, records, minutes, dossiers, and documents. He measures progress by economic development through slavery, as proven by statistics and graphs. Fittingly, he is ousted by clever trickery and a single word from Caspian. Lewis believed that no one is fit to own or dominate another person.

Although the Dufflepuds are probably based on a fabulous medieval creature, they too are some of Lewis's most unforgettable creations. As Lewis's own drawing showed, they are like mushrooms with three-foot stalks and an "umbrella" attached to each. Each Dufflepud has one thick leg under the body. At the end of it is one enormous foot—"a broad-toed foot with the toes curling up a little so that it looked rather like a small canoe." The foot keeps off sun and rain, can be used as a boat, and bounces them up and down like a spring.

A "duffer" appropriately means an incapable, foolish, stupid, inept, unproductive person. Once dwarfs and servants of Coriakin the Magician, they disobeyed his reasonable request that they obtain water from a nearby stream instead of trudging half a mile away to a spring. Conceited and illogical, they wash dishes before dinner and plant boiled potatoes to save time. They constantly repeat every trivial and obvious pronouncement from their Chief. Coriakin, who because of their illogic, must rule by rough magic and not by wisdom, is being punished for something he did and is in charge of them. He puts an "uglifying spell" on them. To avoid seeing each other's ugliness, they put a spell on each other, making themselves invisible. And, of course, Lucy makes them visible again, at their request.

One can't help seeing in the Duffllepuds a little of man's own relationship to God. Although the Magician wants the best for them, they persist in going their own foolish ways or changing what they are for something worse. Instead of allowing Coriakin to rule them by wisdom, they view him in all the wrong ways. At times, they believe he is powerful and dangerous; at other times, they believe they can fool him with tricks.

Narrative

The Chronicles primarily use narrative ("this story is about") and dialogue. An omniscient narrator tells the story, but this perspective sometimes changes when the story is told from a character's point of view (e.g. Lucy, Edmund, Eustace, Trumpkin, Emeth, the Hermit). At other times, the narrator says he won't have the character tell the story, such as when he does not use the dwarf's words but only "the gist." Some details have been obtained from the characters themselves. The narrator often comments on events ("I agree with them" or "Now we come to one of the nastiest things in the story").

In general, Lewis uses short sentences and a conversational style, mentioning himself ("I" or "we") or addressing the reader ("you"). He often interrupts the narrative by addressing the reader. For example, he says you need to know port and starboard, or he asks, "Have you ever. . . ?"

The narrator also comments about his telling of the story. For example, he tells us he may explain about the islands in another book or that he had better finish the story of Rabadash. He says he could write pages and pages but "I will skip on," "I haven't time to tell it now," it would be dull to write down the details, or the story is almost over.

The narrator especially has trouble describing Aslan's country:

> It is as hard to explain how this sunlit land was different from the old Narnia, as it would be to tell you how the fruits of that country taste. . . . I can't describe it any better than that . . . the things that began to happen after that were so great and beautiful that I cannot write them.

Description and Language

Lewis says that in writing the books, he first saw images, then they sorted themselves into events by becoming a story. They didn't have a "love interest" or "close psychology" (*On Stories* 46). The type of literature that seemed appropriate was the fairy tale. The fairy tale is brief, contains little description, uses a limited vocabulary, and has "flexible traditionalism" and "inflexible hostility" to analysis and digression (46). In one of his letters to a child, Lewis gives advice about other characteristics of good writing (*Letters to Children* 64).

Describe things rather than using adjectives that tell us how to feel. The writer, Lewis suggests, must not rely on adjectives or adverbs but rather must make readers feel. The art lies in "making us believe we have imagined the unimaginable" (*Discarded* 207). For example, rather than say something is "delightful," make us say that once we've read the passage.

The narrator tries to convey the joy Lucy and Susan feel in riding on Aslan's back. He asks us to compare it to riding on a galloping horse, then taking away the noise, and then imagining the "soft roughness of golden fur." Next, he asks us to imagine going twice as fast on a mount that never tires and has perfect footing. "And you are riding not on a road nor in a park nor even on the downs but right across Narnia, in spring."

In *The Voyage of the Dawn Treader,* description provides a contrast between good and evil. For example, the narrator describes the sweet smell near the End of the World as not "sleepy or overpowering," but a "fresh, wild, lonely smell that seemed to get into your brain and make you feel that you could go up mountains at a run or wrestle with an elephant." "Whiteness, shot with faintest colour of gold, spread round them on every side." If their eyes had not become so strong, they would have not been able to bear it. They never feel tired. In contrast, the narrator compares the "Darkness" of the Dark Island to the mouth of a railway tunnel: "You could see the water looking pale and grey as it would look late in the evening. But beyond that again, utter blackness as if they had come to the edge of a moonless and starless night." The lights look "lurid and unnatural." The lantern makes a "greasy sort of reflection" in the water, and "the ripple made by their advancing prow appeared to be heavy, small, and lifeless."

Lewis distinguishes between realism of presentation (detail, close-ups, description, minor characters) and realism of content (trueness to life). Realism of presentation involves making the story vivid by "palpable" and "sharp" detail such as the "dragon sniffing along the stone" in *Beowulf* (*Christian* 134).

Like many fairy stories, Lewis's style is remarkably clear and vivid. The narrator describes smells, sounds, and touch, such as the "crunch-crunch" of the snow or "the hissing, and delicious smell of sausages, and more, and more, and more sausages. . . . real meaty, spicey ones, fat and piping hot and burst and just the tiniest bit burnt." He often provides the tiniest details, down to the dead bluebottle on the window-sill, the slight blister on Susan's heel, or Lucy's arm feeling "dead" from being in one position too long.

He also gives practical advice, such as Mrs. Beaver remembering to bring the bread-knife or being able to climb a slippery slope if you use your hands as well as your feet. In fact, Lewis was concerned about the accuracy of the books, such as the type of fire a Marshwiggle could put out with webbed feet (Hooper, *C.S. Lewis* 404). Often, the narrator repeats details, such as it being silly to shut the wardrobe door. He also uses similes such as the statues coming back to life like burning newspaper or towers on the castle that look like dunce's or sorcerer's caps. Foreshadowing is used when he compares the children's coats from the wardrobe to royal robes.

Lewis advises that you should write with the ear as if the story is being read aloud. He is especially fond of describing meals. Who can forget the many, long-awaited meals the Pevensie children sit down to eat—the "nice brown eggs, lightly boiled . . . sardines on toast, and then buttered toast, and then toast with honey, and then a sugar topped cake" with Mr. Tumnus; or the freshly caught trout, boiled potatoes, and sticky marmalade rolls with the Beavers; or the turkeys, geese, peacocks, boar's heads, sides of venison, pies shaped like ships or dragons or elephants, ice puddings, bright lobsters, gleaming salmon, nuts, grapes, pineapples, peaches, pomegranates, melons, and tomatoes at Aslan's Table? Lewis uses lists like this quite frequently, such as the items in the Beaver's house or treasures in ruins of Cair Paravel.

Make sentences so clear that it is obvious what you mean. Lewis generally uses simple sentence structure and fairly short sentences. However, there are occasional long sentences used primarily when the narrator builds up lists of items. For example, in *The Lion*, when the narrator describes the Faun's tales of life in the forest, one sentence is over 116 words long! Lewis effectively uses these long sentences— usually by connecting words with "and," "or," "but"— to convey to us joy or other sensations. For example, in describing Aslan's face, the narrator writes:

> the face seemed to be a sea of tossing gold in which they were floating, and such a sweetness and power rolled about them and over them and entered into them that they felt they had never really been happy or wise or good, or even alive and awake, before.

Use "plain direct" words rather than "long vague" ones and use concrete nouns. Also use words the same size as the subject. Otherwise, you won't have any words left when you want to describe "something *really* infinite." Detailed and often sensual description can help us visualize heaven's future glory through using forms of beauty and pleasure that convey future apocalyptic splendor. Even details of setting and atmosphere are important, because the landscape parallels the inner spiritual quest.

Images

In *A Preface to Paradise Lost*, Lewis describes Milton's use of images to arouse the reader's imagination rather than simply describe his own. He uses language to control what already exists in our minds. The Narnia books themselves began with images, and Lewis also give us deep, unforgettable images within the books. Images can make deep spiritual concepts concrete. A perfect example is Eustace's undragoning by the process of peeling away layer after layer of skin—a marvelous picture of salvation and spiritual regeneration.

Lewis associates Aslan and his country with images such as brightness, a fragrant smell, hills, the garden, and the door. The Apple of Life that Digory brings his mother makes everything in our world look "faded and dingy." Its brightness makes you not want to look at anything else. "And the smell of the Apple of Youth was as if there was a window in the room that opened on Heaven."

In *Voyage of the "Dawn Treader,"* the voyage east to the World's End and Aslan's country is both an external and internal voyage. Near the End of the World, the light grows brighter and brighter, the sea smooth and white with lilies, the water clear and luminous like "drinkable light":

> They could see more light than they had ever seen before. And the deck and the sail and their own faces and bodies became brighter and brighter and every rope shone. . . . Every day and every hour the light became more brilliant and still they could bear it.

Besides fairy tale, an important influence on the form, themes and images is the Bible itself. The Bible is thus the source of many of the images used in fantasy, such as blood, dragons and beasts, light and darkness, sun, water, sea, river and fountain, gold, the city, birds, garden, tree, purifying fire, sinister forest, music, and cave. In addition, the inner world is made real and personal by giving it concrete form through characters and actions. Christ is the epic hero returning on a white horse to slay the dragon, Satan, defeat evil, and become King (Revelation 19:11-16). In later chapters, we will look further at Lewis's use of images. But first, we will look in more detail at Lewis's use of fairy tale heroes.

Seeing Man as Hero

3

"Man as a whole, Man pitted against the universe,
have we seen him at all till we see that he is like a hero in a fairy tale?"
On Stories 89

Sons of Adam and Daughters of Eve

The previous chapters have shown how Lewis came to write the Chronicles and selected the fairy tale as the best form for his story. In addition to elements such as secondary world, magic, and fairy tale style, Lewis uses child heroes. Again, Lewis believed a "never-never land" was appropriate for making a serious comment about the real life of humans: "Man as a whole, Man pitted against the universe, have we seen him at all till we see that he is like a hero in a fairy tale?" (*On Stories* 89).

Fairy tale heroes are traditionally flat and undeveloped. While heroes may be traditional superheroes, they are children—including females—and even animals and other creatures. For example, Reepicheep is the epitome of the chivalrous hero. Lewis advises that the more "unusual" the scenes and events, the more "ordinary" and "typical" the characters should be. This element not only conveys a positive view of man but also shows that the most insignificant person can be a hero.

The basic plot of secondary world fantasy is that of an ordinary hero who undergoes adventures in a strange landscape. He or she has a goal or quest, such as a foe to overcome or a person to be found, undergoes a series of tests or obstacles, and eventually restores order. The ending often results in the child becoming royalty. The Pevensie children and Caspian, Rilian, and Shasta all portray these qualities. In addition, Lewis depicts strong female heroines, such as Lucy, Aravis, Polly, and Jill.

Physical strength, courage, resourcefulness, and morality may be tested, while negative characters may need to be converted or expelled. The quest is typically symbolic of an inner journey—usually one's search for God or one's identity. One of the most important results of the spiritual journey is an inner change in the characters and, in turn, the reader. A major theme throughout the Chronicles, then, is the growth of the heroes.

Digory Kirke (1888-1949)

In *The Magician's Nephew*, twelve-year-old Digory Kirke is living in London with his Aunt and Uncle Ketterley because his father is away in India and his mother is dying. In his misery, he befriends Polly Plummer, and they explore the Ketterley house.

When his Uncle Andrew, a dabbler in magic, sends Polly to another world with a magic ring, Digory sees through his evil nature and sets off to rescue Polly. When they enter the dead world of Charn, he is wildly curious about what will happen if he strikes a bell because he is "the sort of person who wants to know everything." The bell awakens the evil Jadis, who overpowers Digory with her beauty. Although Jadis accidently returns to London and wreaks havoc, Digory manages to send her to Narnia as Aslan is just creating it.

Although Digory is awed by Aslan, he bravely steps forward to speak to him about helping his mother. But when Aslan questions him about the Witch, Digory admits he woke her up.

After he asks Polly to forgive him, Digory is sent to get an apple for Aslan, even though he had hoped to get help for his mother in exchange. "He didn't know how it was to be done but he felt quite sure now that he would be able to do it" because Aslan's kiss gives him "new strength and courage." He is also given Fledge, the first winged horse, as an aid, as well as certain signs to look for.

He must enter the garden alone. There the Witch tempts him to eat one apple in order to avoid missing out on some knowledge that will make him happy all his life or to take an apple home to his mother. He knows "that the most terrible choice lay before him." Although he has been taught not to steal or break promises, the Witch's suggestion that he leave Polly behind makes him see the falseness of the witch's arguments. Despite the success of his quest, Digory is sad and unsure "that he had done the right thing: but whenever he remembered the shining tears in Aslan's eyes he became sure." When Aslan praises him, Digory does not feel conceited but content. He is rewarded with an apple for his mother because he did not insist on stealing it of his own will.

By 1940, when the Pevensie children come to stay with him, he is "the famous professor Kirke" still living in the grand old country house. He has shaggy white hair on his face as well as his head, and he is so odd looking the children have to stifle laughs. His house is a tourist attraction ten miles from the nearest train station and two miles from a post office. He owns the Ketterley House, too. He has no wife, only a housekeeper and three servants.

When the special Narnian tree he had planted blew down in a storm, he made a wardrobe from the wood, which he now keeps in his country home. By 1942, however, he has become so poor that he has to live in a small cottage and tutor students like Peter to make a living. Then seven years later, as a result of a "reunion" he holds for friends of Narnia, he and the others end up in a fatal train accident. His golden beard flows over his chest, and his face is "full of wisdom."

Polly Plummer (1889-1949)

Eleven-year old Polly Plummer is outspoken, curious, practical, and sensitive. When she first meets Digory, she says his name is funny and that he needs to wash his face. She responds indignantly when he calls London a "hole." Yet she humbly apologizes when Digory tells her his mother is ill. She explores the attic of her house and creates a secret room containing her treasures and writes stories. In contrast to Digory, Polly absolutely refuses to do any exploring in new worlds until she makes sure about getting back to the old one: "She was quite as brave as he about some dangers . . . but she was not so interested in finding out things nobody had ever heard of."

Polly seems more sensible than Digory, marking the pool in the Wood Between the Worlds so they can find their way back home. She warns Digory not to ring the bell and immediately dislikes the Witch. In addition, she insists on going with Digory to get the apple and refuses to leave him when there is no food. But she stays out of the argument in the garden because "it wasn't 'her' mother who was dying."

Peter Pevensie (1927-1949)

At thirteen, Peter is the oldest of the four children and thus is given the most responsibility. He apologizes, for example, for disbelieving Lucy and is willing to accept the blame for Edmund's treachery: "That was partly my fault, Aslan. I was angry with him and I think that helped him to go wrong."

Aslan tells Peter he will be High King and in charge of the battle against the Witch. But he discovers the inner resources to come through despite his fears: "He did not feel very brave; indeed, he felt he was going to be sick. But that made no difference to what he had to do." Aslan strikes him with the flat of his sword and calls him Sir

Peter Fenris-Bane. After the battle, Lucy notices that Peter looks strangely pale, stern, and seems so much older.

Peter becomes High King of Narnia—"Peter the Magnificent." He is described as a great deep-chested leader and warrior. Thus his sword Rhindon is an appropriate gift. Peter exemplifies the true chivalric ideal because he tempers his courage with courtesy and fair-mindedness, refusing, for example, to kill Miraz when he has the advantage.

In *The Last Battle*, Peter locks the Door on the old Narnia with a golden key. It is possible that Lewis appropriately named him after Peter, the "rock" upon whom Christ builds his church, and who is given the keys to the kingdom.

Lucy Pevensie (1932-1949)

"Gay and golden haired" Lucy, eight, is one of the most clearly depicted characters in all the Narnia books—perhaps because she spends more time in Narnia than any other child. Lucy becomes "The Valiant" as a Queen in Narnia. When the children become rulers and go to war, Lucy is described as being "as good as a man, or at any rate as good as a boy."

As the first to discover Narnia through the wardrobe, she feels frightened and yet inquisitive and excited. Even though her siblings doubt that she has been to Narnia, they admit that she is usually truthful and reliable. Because Lucy seems to be the most sensitive and caring of all the children, her gift of healing cordial is appropriate. For example, when Mr. Tumnus is captured by the Witch for hiding her, Lucy feels responsible and determines to rescue him. In *The Horse and His Boy*, Lucy's conscience makes her check on the disagreeable

Eustace when he is seasick. In contrast to Eustace, who despises the voyage, Lucy thinks she is "the most fortunate girl in the world." She also shares some of her water ration with him and is the first one to sense his hurt and help him after he becomes a dragon.

On the Island of the Voices in *The Voyage of the "Dawn Treader,"* she tactfully tries to convince the Dufflepuds they aren't ugly. She is the one the Dufflepuds choose to find the spell in the Magic Book so they will be visible again. At first tempted to try the spell that makes you beautiful beyond the lot of mortals, she chooses instead the one that lets you know what your friends think

> "Then her face lit up till, for a moment ... she looked almost as beautiful as that other Lucy in the picture, and she ran forward with a little cry of delight and with her arms stretched out. For what stood in the doorway was Aslan himself. . ."
> The Voyage of the "Dawn Treader"

of you because she is insecure. When she is horrified by what her friend says, Aslan tells her she was spying and has misjudged her friend, thus spoiling potential friendship. She also feels guilty for having left her friends so long. Despite her insecurity, she makes friends easily, as seen in her instant bond with Mr. Tumnus and the sea girl.

Lucy seems to be closer to Aslan than anyone else. Sensing that something will happen to Aslan, Lucy and Susan keep him company on the night of his death and secretly watch his murder. Then they joyfully romp with him after he is resurrected.

In *Prince Caspian*, during the children's long trek with Caspian to Aslan's How, Lucy is the first one who is able to see Aslan when they are lost. She is not only the most sensitive to Aslan's will, but also the children's faith determines when and how they see Aslan. Aslan's voice, which she has been longing for, is the one she loves best in the world: "She rushed to him. She felt her heart would burst if she lost a moment." One stern look from Aslan makes her realize it was her responsibility to follow him, despite the others: "It wasn't my fault anyway, was it?. . . Don't look at me like that. . . oh well, I suppose I *could*." She is instructed to make the others follow him even though they don't believe her. "Now you are a lioness," says Aslan, "And now all Narnia will be renewed." She also learns that he will seem bigger to her every year she grows bigger.

We can understand why, at the end of *The Last Battle*, during all the final indescribable events in Aslan's country, Lucy silently "drinks in" everything more deeply than the others.

Susan Pevensie (1928-1949)

Susan, twelve, is the pretty, tenderhearted one in the family. Although she acts old for her age, she is poor at school work. Because she is skilled at archery and swimming, her gift of arrows is appropriate. She becomes Susan the Gentle as Queen of Narnia. A tall, gracious, tender-hearted woman with black hair that almost reaches the ground, Susan is known for her beauty. Kings of the countries beyond the sea send ambassadors asking for her hand in marriage. In fact, Prince Rabadash's vicious attack on Archenland in *The Horse and His Boy* is triggered by his irrational passion to marry and avenge her. When the children become rulers, Susan does not ride to wars.

In *Prince Caspian,* she is the last of the children to see Aslan because, she says, she didn't let herself believe. Lucy persuades the group to follow Aslan although no one else can see him. But Susan later admits, "I really believed it was him. . . deep down inside. Or I could have, if I'd let myself."

One of the most perplexing and disappointing details of all the stories is that in the end Susan is denied admittance to Aslan's country because she is "no longer a friend of Narnia." Eustace says that during the final days, whenever anyone tried to talk to her about Narnia, she said, "What wonderful memories you have! Fancy your still thinking about all those funny games we used to play when we were children." She becomes interested in "grown-up" things such as lipstick and nylons. Jill says, "She always was a jolly sight too keen on being grown-up." "Grownup, indeed," replies Polly. "I wish she *would* grow up. . . . Her whole idea is to race on to the silliest time of one's life as quick as she can and then stop there as long as she can."

Susan is perhaps symbolic of the superficial Christian whose commitment is too shallow to be real. We can assume that she never really believed in Aslan in her heart. Lewis says in a letter that there is time for her to mend, and she may get to Aslan's country in her own way (*Letters to Children* 67).

Edmund Pevensie (1930-1949)

Edmund, ten, is known as a traitor. He is skeptical, spiteful, and difficult to get along with, especially with Peter and Susan. Although Lucy is his favorite sibling, he denies that he has been to Narnia with Lucy. Returning from his solo visit to Narnia, he grows increasingly nasty and spiteful and even lies about having been there. He does not receive a gift from Father Christmas because he is under the White Witch's control.

Edmund commits treachery by succumbing to the Witch's temptation. Although he knows "deep down inside" that the White Witch is "bad and cruel," he wants to become King. Although he fears the Witch's house, he mocks and disfigures the statue of the lion and jeers at what he thinks is "silly old Aslan." Yet when he sees the animals turned to stone, for the first time he feels sorry for someone else. When the Witch begins to mistreat him and he finds himself being bound as a victim for the Stone Table, he begins to admit the truth to himself.

Although Edmund is a seemingly unworthy person, Aslan, who sees the worth of every individual, sacrifices himself in Edmund's place. Edmund's transformation after he realizes the evil nature of the Witch—whom he really believed was bad all along—is remarkable. He and Aslan stroll together alone, and although no one hears what Aslan says, "it was a conversation which Edmund never forgot." Edmund had gotten "past thinking about himself after all he'd been through and after the talk he'd had that morning. He just went on looking at Aslan." Edmund may never have fully realized what Aslan did for him—"it would be too awful. . . . Think how you'd feel if you were he."

Edmund plays a key role in fighting the Witch by breaking her wand. Although he is wounded in battle, Lucy heals him with her cordial. As King, Edmund appropriately becomes a more grave and quiet man than Peter and so great in council and judgment that he is called King Edmund the Just. When he returns from Narnia, he is his "real old self again and could look you in the face."

When he returns to Narnia in *Prince Caspian*, Ed is the first to feel the pull back into Narnia, and he is relieved to be back rather than on a train back to school. He insists on exploring the woods and the ruins of Cair Paravel. He is also the first to recognize that time has passed in Narnia. When Lucy sees Aslan, Edmund—remembering his treachery—votes to believe Lucy: "I was worst of the lot, I know. Yet she was right after all. Wouldn't it be fair to believe her this time?"

Edmund's experience as a reformed traitor makes him sympathetic with others. It is fitting that during the later adventure of the "Dawn Treader," he chastizes Caspian for being greedy and is skeptical about Ramandu's daughter. When Eustace describes his "undragoning" to Edmund, Ed admits, "You haven't been as bad as I was on my first trip to Narnia. You were only an ass, but I was a traitor." Likewise, in *The Horse and His Boy*, Edmund empathizes with Shasta, who feels like a traitor for eavesdropping. Edmund lays his hand on Shasta's head: "I know now that you were no traitor, boy."

Eustace Clarence Scrubb (1933-1949)

Eustace, the Pevensies' cousin, "half-deserved the name," says Lewis. At the beginning of *The Voyage of the "Dawn Treader,"* Eustace is a selfish, lazy, puny, bossy bully with no friends, who tries to impress others with his infinite superiority. His "up-to-date" and "advanced" family includes Harold and Alberta, whom Eustace calls by their first names. They are vegetarians, non-smokers, and teetotalers; wear special underclothes; have little furniture; and sleep with the windows open. Even after

> "He had turned into a dragon while he was asleep. Sleeping on a dragon's hoard with greedy, dragonish thoughts in his heart, he had become a dragon himself."
>
> *The Voyage of the "Dawn Treader"*

Eustace changes for the better, his mother insists that he has become "tiresome and commonplace."

His diary of the voyage presents an excellent insight into his self-centeredness and stupidity: "I have had a ghastly time. . . . It would be bad enough even if one was with decent people instead of fiends in human form. Caspian and Edmund are simply brutal to me." He believes that everyone is against him, despises the food and "primitive" accommodations, has a run-in with Reepicheep—"that little brute"—and all the while deceives himself into thinking he is being considerate. We can just hear him ranting about pacifism, "art," "Plumptree's Vitaminised Nerve Food," and "lodging a disposition" against his companions with the British Consul. How like Eustace to think Calormen the "least phony" of all the countries.

His *inner* change comes on Dragon Island when he sets off alone, trying to escape work. But he doesn't enjoy himself for long. His greediness and inner nastiness are made tangible and visible by his transformation into a dragon. Yet the experience vastly improves him. Realizing the nuisance he has been, he begins to examine his thoughts about himself and the others. For the first time in his life he becomes lonely—a monster cut off from people.

No matter how despicable Eustace is, he can't help but be changed by Narnia. Physically, "his new life, little as he suspected it, had already done him some good." Then Aslan gets hold of him and "from that time forth," Eustace really begins to be a different boy. The change doesn't occur overnight. He had relapses, but "the cure had begun." "Aslan knows me," he says.

Jill Pole (1933-1949)

In *The Silver Chair*, Eustace appears again, this time accompanying Jill Pole on a quest. Jill, who is bullied by her schoolmates at a school called Experiment House, tries to get into Narnia first by magic, then by praying to Aslan. But she is actually called to Narnia to help find the lost Prince Rilian. She and Eustace are guided on this quest by four Signs they must remember by saying them often.

But the children do not obey Aslan's commands or stick to the mission. Instead, they are lured by the beauty of the Witch disguised as a green lady and by the food and shelter of the giant's city. It is their pessimistic Marshwiggle companion Puddleglum who reminds them to have faith and keep going. Ironically, it is also he who gives them most comfort when in the Witch's Underland because he perceives the falseness of her temptation to make their world seem like a dream.

When Jill sees Aslan, she remembers only "how she had helped to muff nearly all the Signs, and about all the snappings and quarrellings. And she wanted to say 'I'm sorry' but she could not speak." But Aslan tells her not to think about it: "I will not always be scolding. You have done the work for which I sent you into Narnia." Thus she and Eustace must return to their world.

Jill and Eustace return to Narnia to aid Tirian in *The Last Battle.* Now sixteen, Jill is an excellent archer and pathfinder because of her experiences in the Northern

Lands. Tirian is amazed "to find how silently and almost invisibly she glided on before them." Jill sneaks inside the Stable and discovers that the false Aslan is only the donkey Puzzle in disguise. Thus Tirian considers her both disobedient and "the bravest and most woodwise of all" his subjects. When he commands them to return home and avoid a bloody end, Jill insists on sticking with him "whatever happens" so they can accept "the adventure that Aslan would send them."

Caspian X

Caspian is the only character whom we follow in several books from childhood to death. A Telmarine, Caspian lives in the castle of King Miraz and his aunt because his parents are dead. His nurse, who teaches him about the Talking Beasts of old Narnia, is dismissed for telling silly stories. His new teacher, the dwarf Doctor Cornelius, continues to secretly tell him about Narnia's happier days before Miraz usurped the throne. Although the dwarf begins to educate Caspian, the boy also learns "a great deal by using his own eyes and ears."

Because Caspian's life is in danger, Cornelius sends the child away, for Caspian is the true king of Narnia, and Miraz's wife has given birth to an heir. The dwarf presents him with Susan's horn, which will call help in time of need. Caspian builds an army of all the beasts of Narnia and uses this horn to call the children back to Narnia.

When Aslan eventually pronounces him King of Narnia, Caspian feels he is insufficient. "I'm only a kid," he says. "Good," says Aslan. "If you had felt yourself sufficient, it would have been a proof that you were not." When Caspian wishes he came of a "more honourable lineage," Aslan assures him that coming from Adam and Eve "is both honour enough to erect the head of the poorest beggar, and shame enough to bow the shoulders of the greatest emperor in earth."

Caspian learns the responsibility of kingship in *The Voyage of the "Dawn Treader"* when he decides to abandon his ship and country and sail with Reepicheep to the East. But Reepicheep reminds him he cannot: "You are the King of Narnia. You break faith with all your subjects. . . if you do not return. You shall not please yourself with adventures as if you were a private person."

Caspian's death in *The Silver Chair* allows the children to learn about the hope of an afterlife. During Caspian's funeral in Narnia, the children are taken to Aslan's Mountain. Eustace is told to drive a thorn into Aslan's paw, and the blood splashes onto Caspian. As death begins to work backward, Caspian leaps up before them. He looks no particular age, just as the children seem neither old nor young. They are promised that they, too, will come here to stay one day.

Shasta and Aravis

The Horse and His Boy centers on two different children, Shasta and Aravis. The central themes of this book include the search for identity and overcoming pride. Shasta lives with the poor fisherman Arsheesh, who discovered him washed to shore in a small boat with a dying knight. When Shasta overhears a Tarkaan offering to buy him as a slave, he is at first relieved he is not related to Arsheesh, whom he has never loved: "Why, I might be anyone!" he thinks. "I might be the son of a Tarkaan myself. . . or of a god!"

Shasta decides to run away to Narnia on a talking horse named Bree, who must teach him about riding and Narnia's wars because Shasta has never read any books.

They join Aravis and her talking horse, Hwin, who are also running away. Aravis's father is lord of Calavar, and her mother is dead. Because her stepmother hates her, she promises Aravis in marriage to Ahoshta, an old and important man. Hwin convinces her not to commit suicide but to run away to Narnia with her.

At first, Shasta and Aravis dislike each other. Although  Aravis is "proud and could be hard enough," she is "as true as steel and would never have deserted a companion, whether she liked him or not." When her friend Lasaraleen teases her about going to Narnia with a peasant boy, Aravis acknowledges, "I'll be a nobody, just like him." It is the Lion, Aslan, who gives Aravis ten scratches on her back. These, he explains later, are equal to the stripes her stepmother whipped into a slave because of her, and she "needed to know what it felt like."

Shasta, on the other hand, believes he is "no one in particular," but his potential surfaces on their journey. When attacked by a lion, for example, he is the only one who is brave. Bree is ashamed "to be beaten by a little human boy—a child, a mere foal, who had never held a sword nor had any good nurture or example in his life!"

Though exhausted and disheartened, Shasta must run alone to warn King Lune about impending attack: "He writhed inside at what seemed the cruelty and unfairness of the demand. He had not yet learned that if you do one good deed your reward usually is to be set to do another and harder and better one." Reaching the mountaintop dripping in fog, Shasta considers himself "the most unfortunate boy that ever lived in the whole world." Then Aslan appears to him and reveals that he has been his guide all along.

King Lune recognizes Shasta as his son Cor, the twin of Prince Corin. Cor has fulfilled a prophecy that he would save Archenland from deadly danger. As the oldest twin, he eventually becomes king, even though he doesn't want to, and marries Aravis. Thus Shasta's story is the typical fairy tale plot: the child departs on a journey, undergoes trials, is revealed to be royalty, is restored to his family, and marries.

Shasta and Bree are opposites, as are Aravis and Hwin. Shasta and Hwin must gain confidence, just as Aravis and Bree are self-centered and patronizing. Acknowledging Shasta's courage, Aravis admits, "I've been snubbing him and looking down on him. . . and now he turns out to be the best of us all." She apologizes to Shasta for her attitude: "I'm sorry I've been such a pig. But I did change before I knew you were a Prince. . . when you went back, and faced the Lion." Bree likewise learns, "as long as you know you're nobody very special, you'll be a very decent sort of Horse."

The Role of Humans

Although humans are not created in Narnia, they nevertheless play an important role there. Aslan usually calls the children from our world into another to perform certain tasks, despite their poor education. However, they also learn moral values such as obedience and resisting temptation that can be applied to our world.

Tasks

The children are "called" into Narnia when there is trouble. Each person in Narnia has a special task to perform—usually something he doesn't want to do. Digory knows he must put on a magic ring and bravely rescue Polly, and he must get the apple. He feels unfit for his task, but with the helpmates provided for him, he achieves his goal and learns to obey. Lucy must help the Dufflepuds; Peter must kill Fenris Ulf, and so on.

Child characters are surprised to find that they have been "called" to another world for a purpose. They are always provided supernatural help through animal or human guides and counsels, provisions, and gifts. In *The Lion*, Father Christmas presents three of the children with special gifts that prove invaluable, even in later adventures. These gifts are appropriate to their personalities and generally reflect the roles each will play in the salvation of Narnia. Each receives two gifts: an item to be used for protection or healing and a weapon.

GIFTS		
CHILD	GIFT OF PROTECTION	GIFT FOR FIGHTING
Peter	shield	sword
Lucy	cordial	dagger
Susan	horn	arrows

Peter receives a shield with a Great Red Lion on it and the sword Rhindon that is "just the right size and weight for Peter to use. Peter was silent and solemn as he received these gifts for he felt they were a very serious kind of present." Lucy receives a small dagger to defend herself if necessary, and a diamond vial containing a cordial that will immediately restore someone who is sick or injured. Susan is given a bow, quiver of arrows and an ivory horn which, if blown, will summon help immediately.

The four Pevensie children are also given new titles:

- Peter the Magnificent
- Susan the Gentle
- Edmund the Just
- Lucy the Valiant

> "Seven Kings and Queens stood before him, all with crowns on their heads and all in glittering clothes."
> *The Last Battle*

Often, the children feel unable to perform the tasks. However, if they keep their eyes on Aslan and not themselves, they find themselves made of sturdier stuff than they ever thought possible. As they develop qualities they never know they had, they discover the ability to use weapons and fight battles. Whatever they take "in hand" as Kings and Queens, they achieve.

The children usually begin to feel stronger, bigger, and more grown up after only a few hours in Narnia: "Once a king or queen in Narnia, always a king or queen." Back in England, they would have never been able to survive such tasks. Every time the children return to Narnia, all their old skills and royal strength are quickly revived because Narnia alters them. In *The Last Battle*, Tirian, for example, is "surprised at the strength of both the children," and they seem "to be already much stronger and bigger and more grown-up than they had been when he first met them a few hours ago."

Just as each child changes in Narnia, no child returns from Narnia unchanged. Polly Plummer, for example, notes how the mysterious tunnels in her house seem tame compared to Charn. Lucy is described as "only one-third of a little girl going to boarding school for the first time, and two-thirds of Queen Lucy of Narnia." Eustace

Scrubb is "inwardly" changed and improved despite his lack of preparation for adventure due to his poor education.

Education

Eustace and his friend Jill Pole provide good examples of what Lewis perceives as dangerous trends in American and British educational systems. They attend Experiment House, a "coeducational" or "mixed" school for both boys and girls. The people with "mixed minds" who run it believe that children should be allowed to do whatever they please. Elsewhere, Lewis attacks so-called "democratic" education that levels courses so that there is less distinction between "intelligent" and "stupid" students and so no one will feel inferior.

At his school, Eustace reads only books of information with "pictures of grain elevators or of fat foreign children doing exercises in model schools." They discuss "exports and imports and governments and drains" in great detail but say little about dragons. Because Eustace has read none of the right books, he has no idea what a dragon is and consequently must turn into one before he learns. These children also have no Bibles, so they don't even know about Adam and Eve. Nor do they have any idea how to tell a story straight, so Eustace has difficulty in describing what happened. Eustace cares only about grades, not about learning a subject for its own sake, and he likes dead beetles pinned to cards.

At the beginning of *The Silver Chair*, Jill and Eustace are so miserable at Experiment House, at the mercy of bullying classmates and subjected to other "horrid things," that they are desperate to escape into Narnia. Not only do they escape, of course, but Aslan also comes back with them to wreak vengeance on the school. Dressed in glittering clothes and with weapons in hand, they return to Experiment House school where Aslan chases out the bullies and the Head: "And from that day forth things changed for the better at Experiment House, and it became quite a good school. And Jill and Eustace were always friends." The Head of Experiment House becomes hysterical and is "made an Inspector to interfere with other Heads." Eventually, she ends up in Parliament, "where she lived happily ever after."

Even in Narnia, though, education can go bad. For example, under Miraz's rule in Narnia, the history taught in schools is "duller than the truest history you ever read." Aslan rescues a poor schoolgirl, Gwendolen, stuck inside a typical girls' school. When the ceiling and walls become trees, Miss Prizzle, a teacher, finds herself standing in a forest: "Then she saw the lion, screamed and fled, and with her fled her class, who were mostly dumpy, prim little girls with fat legs." Even Cor fears that once he is restored to princedom again, "education and all sorts of horrible things" are going to happen to him.

One of the acts of the four Kings and Queens is to free young dwarfs and satyrs from being sent to school. For the children from England, going to Narnia greatly compensates for the faults of their schools. "Why don't they teach logic?" asks Professor Kirke. ""What *do* they teach them at these schools?"

Obedience

In *The Magician's Nephew*, when Aslan calls the Cabby's wife from England, Polly realizes that anyone who heard that call "would want to obey it and (what's more) would be able to obey it, however many worlds and ages lay between." The children learn to obey Aslan and to seek his guidance in all circumstances. In *Prince Caspian* for example, Lucy should have forsaken all the others and come after Aslan alone. Because she didn't, Aslan bids her once more: "You must all get up at once and follow me." Christ also told his disciples, "If anyone wants to be a follower of mine, let him deny himself and take up his cross and follow me," forsaking all else. Later, after learning his lesson, Peter assures Lucy that they cannot know when Aslan will act again, but that nevertheless "he expects us to do what we can on our own."

Digory's first task is simply to help Polly once Andrew sends her off alone. Later, he must abandon his family and follow Aslan at any cost in order to get Aslan the apple. Still, Aslan provides him with help—Fledge and Polly—and special signs to look for—a blue lake, a hill, and a garden. And in reward for obeying and patiently waiting, he is given a healing apple for his mother.

Lucy wishes Aslan will come roaring in and frighten away the enemy. But things never happen the same way twice. She is told in *The Lion* to go save others with her magic cordial and not to stop and wait for Edmund's healing: " 'Wait a minute,' she tells Aslan crossly. 'Daughter of Eve,' said Aslan in a graver voice, 'others also are at the point of death. Must more people die for Edmund?'" When she returns, Edmund looks better than she had ever seen him. So her patience and obedience are rewarded.

Shasta's task is to warn King Lune. Though tired and disheartened, he must continue on alone, and he thinks this is cruel. Often, we feel God is asking us to do more than our share. But, Shasta learns, "if you do one good deed your reward usually is to be set to do another and harder and better one." Likewise, Caspian selfishly, though understandably, wants to abandon his throne in

Narnia, his ship, and his promise to Ramandu's daughter to reach Aslan's country, but he must return at Aslan's bidding.

In *The Silver Chair*, Jill and Eustace are "called" by Aslan out of their world to do an important task. They do not know when Aslan will act. He wants them to do what they can on their own. In their case, Aslan guides them by telling Jill four important Signs she is to follow. Although the Signs are quite clear to her in Aslan's country, he warns her that they will be difficult to recognize in Narnia. So she is to "remember, remember, remember the Signs. Say them to yourself when you wake in the morning and when you lie down at night, and when you wake in the middle of the night." God similarly commanded the Israelites:

> These words which I command you this day shall be upon your heart; and you shall teach them diligently to your children, and shall talk of them when you sit in your house, and when you walk by the way, and when you lie down, and when you rise. And you shall bind them as a sign upon your hand, and they shall be as frontlets between your eyes. (Deuteronomy 6:6-8)

The children, however, don't obey Aslan's commands or stick to their mission. For one thing, they are tempted by food and shelter at Harfang, and thus walk right into a giant trap. Puddleglum must remind them constantly to have faith and to keep going: "Aslan's instructions always work: there are no exceptions." Although it seems illogical, they must obey the Sign and release the seemingly mad Prince even though they are unsure of what he will do. Aslan has told them exactly what to do: untie Rilian. They may even die in the process. But no matter what the consequences, they must obey. "I was going to say I wished we'd never come. But I don't, I don't, I don't. Even if we are killed," Jill proclaims in *The Last Battle*.

Heroes in Religious Fantasy

Religious fantasy can be defined as a work that integrates aspects of Christianity with elements of fantasy. This type of fantasy presents the supernatural world outside our perception as real and credible and humans coming to terms with it. Religious fantasy also presents theological concepts, issues, or moral values. Themes include the importance of the individual, obedience, the inner quest, creation, end times, and the afterlife.

While good versus evil is the plot of most fantasy, in religious fantasy, good wins because God is considered the sovereign and absolute power. Such clear-cut contrasts force the reader to take sides. The hero chooses the side of good, often after an inner battle. This moral struggle is not only the primary focus of the story, but the character's journey is also often symbolic of an inner spiritual quest. Reader identification with this character is thus an effective technique for encouraging changes in the reader's own attitudes and values. For this reason, characters are often converted or morally changed.

Because fantasy encourages the reader to align with a certain character, it is a particularly effective vehicle for presenting moral and spiritual ideas. A reader identifies with characters who are not superheroes but rather common people like ourselves—searching, questioning, and changing. By identifying with such protagonists, the reader, in turn, learns moral values, such as majesty, courtesy, nobility, purity, courage, goodness, sacrifice, and splendor. Because characters undergo a quest or tests, the reader experiences the same things, thus making him act or choose. The story then works on the reader the same way as it works on the characters. In fact, this type of literature has the ability to actually change the reader.

Because many readers might align with an unbeliever, some books contain one or more skeptics who are more resistant to change. Fantasy can thus create the possibility of belief in a skeptic or lead an unbeliever toward belief. In fact, many people have been converted by reading the Narnia Chronicles. Believability is an important quality of the character's change. Otherwise, the story becomes didactic. Rather, it is more effectively conveyed through images and must be integral to the story itself. We will see next how Lewis accomplishes this effect.

Stealing Past Dragons

4

"...supposing that by casting all these things into an imaginary world, stripping them of their stained-glass and Sunday school associations, one could make them for the first time appear in their real potency?
Could one not thus steal past those watchful dragons?"
Of Other Worlds 37

Myth

Lewis said he chose the fairy tale as the ideal form for what he had to say. In the previous chapters, we have looked at the fairy tale form. As fairy tales, the stories contain elements such as a secondary world, magic, talking animals, a simple writing style, and child heroes. In this chapter, we will look at what it was Lewis had to say.

To attract both young and adult readers, a fantasy work must first of all be a good story—a straightforward adventure. Action must be compelling, believable, pleasing, exciting, moving, and relevant. Like all good literature, the story must be interesting and pleasurable rather than exist solely to present truth or philosophy.

The ideal form of fantasy for Lewis is what he called "myth." Whereas myth is usually associated with falsehood, Lewis uses the term differently. In *An Experiment in Criticism*, Lewis explains how myth does not exist in words. First, he tells the basic plot of the Orpheus and Euridice story:

> There was a man who sang and played the harp so well that even beasts and trees crowded to hear him. And when his wife died he went down alive into the land of the dead and made music before the King of the Dead till even he had compassion and gave him back his wife, on condition that he led her up out of that land without once looking back to see her until they came out into the light. But when they were nearly out one moment too soon, the man looked back, and she vanished from him forever (40).

He then gives the mere plot summaries of two other stories. The Orpheus story makes a powerful impression on most readers by making them feel the story's inherent quality. But the other two are dull and boring.

The appeal of the Orpheus story is something beyond its literary form because just the plot can strike us and move us deeply. Lewis considered the plot "a net whereby to catch something else. . . like a state or quality," such as "giantship, otherness, the desolation of space" and the numinous (*On Stories* 17). A good work, he argues, is more than just what happened, because a reader can re-read it and still be moved. Lewis says that you can read a good book a number of times and find more in it, as well as continued delight. This quality is often achieved when there are deeper levels of meaning to be found in statements, action, images, and so forth.

Ideally, the story itself conveys ideas that apply to our "real" world. Even though the work may contain an imaginary world, the meaning is considered true. However, the "message" is conveyed through fantasy and Biblical images, symbols, characters, and events. Because the imagination is considered a better source of images than the natural world, spiritual truths and religious beliefs are transferred or "transposed" into objective devices of fantasy literature: secondary worlds, talking animals, magic, and so on.

One of the chief reasons for Lewis's conversion to Christianity was his realization that it is impossible to perceive reality apart from experiencing it. Once we examine our experience of reality, we are cut off from the object and left with only an abstraction, a mental construct. Lewis believed that the only way to unite reason and imagination is to see every object in its relevant context through metaphor. For Lewis, the most perfect form of metaphor, and thus the closes approach to truth, is myth. We must thus combine reason with imagination to come close to understanding what is real.

Myth is shown to point to what is objectively real, things more solid. Narnia, as Aslan first creates it, makes our world seem "hard and cruel" in comparison. For Narnia is a country of walking trees, visible naiads and dryads in the streams and trees, fauns and satyrs, dwarfs, giants, centaurs and Talking Beasts. The existence of mythological creatures such as these in Narnia grows out of an intriguing idea that occurs quite frequently in Lewis's works—that what is myth and legend in our world may be factual reality in another. Even Bacchus, the Greek god of wine, is seen romping through Narnia, changing the streams to wine. One of the books in Mr. Tumnus' home is titled, with faun humor, "Is Man a Myth?"

But it is difficult to integrate idea and effect so that the meaning emerges with didacticism. For example, fairy tales and children's literature of the Victorian period are noted for their moralizing. For the moral to be one with the story, the theology must be presented through narrative action and embodied in situations so the work maintains its dramatic quality and is not "preachy." It is also desirable that spiritual qualities be shown working through people rather than using characters as personifications. Good and evil can also be illustrated by the characters' behavior.

Because fantasy should be read primarily for pleasure and not edification, every reader will get different meanings depending on his spiritual background, nature, and development. According to Lewis, the moral should arise from the "cast" of the author's mind, as well as "whatever spiritual roots you have succeeded in striking during the whole course of your life. But if they don't show you any moral, don't put one in" (*On Stories* 41-2). When one child called his books "silly stories" without a point, Lewis replied that "looking for a point" may keep a reader from "getting the real effect of the story itself" (*Letters to Children* 35-6). The goal is to convey meaning without rational explanation so that the message or religious echoes wake up things already in the reader. Like a picture, says Lewis, the story should trigger the reader's imagination and emotion.

Many readers cannot help but notice how Aslan "reminds" them of Christ, or how the stories "teach" them certain religious values. In fact, a monk named Brother Stanislas wrote to the New York C. S. Lewis Society that he had read the Narnia tales three times in three years. "They have been for me about the most spiritual books I have read in my 16 years as a monk," he commented. Lewis agreed with a child who called the Narnia books "better than the tracts" (*Letters to Children* 36). But did Lewis intentionally include these theological elements in the stories?

Allegory

There is a fine line between conveying ideas and using obvious allegory. Allegory is a story in which there is a one-to-one correlation between characters or events and a single abstract meaning such as psychological or spiritual experiences that they represent. The author intentionally plans these correspondences between the real and the immaterial or intangible. Lewis describes allegory as a "puzzle with a solution" (*Letters to Children* 81). He wrote to a group of fifth graders that they were wrong in thinking that everything in the Narnia tales "represents" something in the real world as in *Pilgrim's Progress*, an allegory by John Bunyan. But he grants that any story can be interpreted allegorically if the reader tries hard enough.

Lewis claims that in writing his Narnia tales he never consciously started with the moral or didactic purpose of conveying Christian principles. He argues that some people seem to think he first asked how he could talk about Christianity to children, decided on fairy tale as the appropriate form, gathered information from child psychology, selected an age group, listed basic Christian truths, then "hammered out 'allegories' to embody them. This is all pure moonshine." Rather, the Christian element "pushed itself in of its own accord" (*On Stories* 46).

Lewis claims the Christian elements welled up unconsciously into the narrative as he wrote it. When he started *The Lion*, he didn't foresee what Aslan was going to do and suffer. On the other hand, he does admit that the series as a whole became Christian. In *The Magician's Nephew*, for example, Aslan creates Narnia. In *Prince Caspian*, old stories about Aslan are starting to be disbelieved. At end of *The Voyage of the "Dawn Treader,"* Aslan appears as a Lamb. His three replies to Shasta suggest the Trinity. In *The Silver Chair*, the old king is raised from the dead by a drop of Aslan's blood. *The Last Battle* describes the reign of the anti-Christ (ape), the end of the world, and the Last Judgment (*Letters* 486). Walter Hooper suggests that "'disguise' of a sort was part of Lewis' intention" (*Past* 106). Lewis was convinced that any amount of theology can be smuggled into people's minds "under the cover of romance" without their knowing it.

According to Lewis, he was not *exactly* representing the real Christian story in symbols but rather things in his book are "like" Biblical ones or may "remind" us of them (Hooper, *Past* 109-110). Consequently, we will not find a one-to-one relationship between stories and the Bible because he did not intend for us to. Walter Hooper warns that trying to explain stories such as the Narnia Chronicles as one would decipher a code destroys their very purpose, so we should not search for analogies too closely or expect to find them. Lewis gives advice on the dangers to trying to find parallels: "Within a given story any object, person, or place is neither more nor less than what the story effectively shows it to be" (*Studies* 39-40).

Although Biblical principles are very much present in the Narnia series, they are certainly not allegory. If one tries to find such correspondences—for example, a comparison of Aslan's sacrifice with Christ's crucifixion—he will be disappointed. The Narnia tales cannot be taught as a kind of systematic theology because there are not exact parallels between the Bible and Narnia. Aslan does not represent the Son of God incarnate as a Lion. In addition, there is no doctrine of Atonement in Narnia because Aslan is sacrificed for only one boy. Sometimes it is not until later that the two worlds are joined in the mind. Artist Pauline Baynes, for example, told Hooper that she was moved by Aslan's sacrifice but did not realize who he was meant to be until after she had illustrated *The Lion, the Witch and the Wardrobe*. What makes the Narnia books Christian are the moral themes that are part of the narrative rather than Biblical echoes.

Lewis believed that a writer, as "creator" in a sense, "rearranges" elements God has already provided in his world and which already contain his meanings. George MacDonald, a writer who greatly influenced Lewis, explains this process in his essay on "The Fantastic Imagination":

> One difference between God's work and man's is, that, while God's work cannot mean more than he meant, man's must mean more than he meant. For in everything that God has made, there is layer upon layer of ascending significance; also he expresses the same thought in higher and higher kinds of that thought: it is God's things, his embodied thoughts, which alone a man has to use, modified and adapted to his own purposes, for the expression of his thoughts; therefore he cannot help his words and figures falling into such combinations in the mind of another as he had him-self not foreseen, so many are the thoughts allied to every other

thought, so many are the relations involved in every figure, so many the facts in every symbol. (27)

Tolkien thought the Christian meaning in the Narnia books was too obvious. Because sometimes the Christian allusion in Lewis's books becomes too didactic, he is noted for making his fiction a formal apology for Christianity.

Supposition

Lewis distinguishes allegory from "supposition." Each mixes the real and unreal in different ways. For example, in Bunyan's *Pilgrim's Progress*, the giant represents despair. In contrast, when ideas are "supposed," we can see them in new ways. The story exists even if we remove the theological elements (*Letters* 475-6). Lewis points out, "It would be rather a tall order to have a story strictly about God (beginning, 'One day God decided'. . .) but to imagine what God might be supposed to have done in other worlds does not seem to be wrong" (*Letters* 446).

In a letter to a little girl, Lewis wrote,

> I'm not exactly "representing" the real (Christian) story in symbols. I'm more saying, "Suppose there were a world like Narnia and it needed rescuing and the Son of God (or the Great Emperor Over-sea) went to redeem it, as He came to redeem ours, what might, in that world, all have been like?" (*Letters to Children* 92)

He adds that the creation of Narnia is "the Son of God creating *a* world." Although Jadis plucks the apple in disobedience, she was already fallen. The Stone Table is a reminder of Moses' table. Aslan's passion and resurrection are similar to those in our world but not exactly. Edmund is a "sneak and traitor" like Judas, but he repents and is forgiven. Aslan does appear more like

Christ at the End of the World, especially when he is a Lamb. Finally, Ape and Puzzle are similar to Antichrist (*Letters to Children* 92-3).

In a letter to Anne (March 5, 1961), Lewis provides much insight into what he believes the books are about. He says that there is a "deeper meaning" behind *The Lion.* "The whole Narnian story is about Christ." The stories are his answer to supposing what would happen if a world like Narnia went wrong and Christ went there to save it. Lewis says Aslan is a Talking Beast because "Narnia is a world of Talking Beasts." He also pictured Aslan as a lion because "(a) the lion is supposed to be the king of beasts; (b) Christ is called 'the Lion of Judah' in the Bible; (c) I'd been having strange dreams about lions when I began writing the work" (Hooper, *C.S. Lewis* 426).

> "Wrong will be right, when Aslan comes in sight,
> At the sound of his roar, sorrows will be no more,
> When he bares his teeth, winter meets its death
> And when he shakes his mane, we shall have spring again."
>
> *The Lion, the Witch and the Wardrobe*

Furthermore, Lewis goes on to explain what each book in the series is about:

The Magician's Nephew is about Narnia's creation and evil entering it.

The Lion is about "the Crucifixion and Resurrection."

Prince Caspian is about "restoration of the true religion after corruption."

The Horse and His Boy is about "the calling and conversion of a heathen."

The Voyage of the "Dawn Treader" is about "the spiritual life (especially in Reepicheep)."

The Last Battle is about "the coming of the Antichrist (the Ape), the end of the world, and the Last Judgement" (426).

Lewis's goal was to strip the Christian message of its "stained-glass and Sunday school associations" and give it new form and meaning by putting all these things into an imaginary world (*On Stories* 47). By stealing past inhibitions and traditional religious concepts and terminology, he could make them, for the first time, "appear in their real potency." Before Lewis became converted to Christianity, he found certain expressions silly or shocking. Yet he did not mind the same ideas in story or mythic form because he was prepared to feel the myth's profound and suggestive meaning. Although we often feel that we ought to feel a certain way about God, "obligation to feel can freeze feelings."

Aslan

Aslan is an invention that gives an imaginary answer to the question, "What might Christ become like if there really were a world like Narnia and He chose to be incarnate and die and rise again in that world as He actually has done in ours?" (*Letters* 475) In the form of a Lion, Aslan can portray certain qualities of Christ: he is awesome, solemn, stern, and compassionate, and a "terrible good." This technique leads us to a clearer knowledge and understanding of Christ.

Aslan says to King Frank, "You know [me] better than you think you know, and you shall live to know me better yet." And at the end of *The Voyage of the "Dawn Treader,"* Aslan, who has nine names in Narnia, says that in England he has a different name: "You must learn to know me by that name. This was the very reason why you were brought to Narnia, that by knowing me here for a little, you may know me better there." In addition, he no longer looks to them like a lion. Lewis wrote to Lucy Barfield that he was humbled that Aslan allowed him to make Him more real to her (*Letters to Children* 75). In fact, in several of his letters, Lewis seems to equate Aslan with Christ (e.g. "Aslan has done great things for us").

In his *Preface to Paradise Lost,* Lewis says it is hard to draw interesting, convincing, good characters like Aslan, who are better than yourself. To see a person inferior to yourself, all you have to do is stop doing something, such as being vain, greedy, cruel, or envious. But Lewis says to portray a better person involves imagining and prolonging the very best moments you have had. Because we regretfully do not know what it feels like to be good, such characters usually end up like puppets and uninteresting because they are not individuals. But if he could only partially succeed, Lewis believed it worth doing (100-1).

Who is Aslan?

The one person who makes Narnia worth visiting is Aslan himself— "It isn't Narnia, you know," sobbed Lucy. "It's you." Aslan, of course, is the Great Lion, Son of the Emperor-Beyond-the-Sea, King above all High Kings, King of the Wood and Beasts, Maker of the Stars. Aslan is the only character who appears in all seven of the Narnia books. He doesn't actually reside in Narnia but rather comes and goes in other worlds: "One day you'll see him and another you won't. He doesn't like being tied down, and of course he has other countries to attend to." There are 100 years, for example, when the Witch rules in perpetual Narnian winter, and Christmas never comes. Caspian and Tirian have real difficulty believing in Aslan because they have only heard legends about him.

Many readers sense that Aslan is a "divine" or "Christlike" figure. As mentioned before, if readers do not see Aslan in this way, Lewis would not want them to, because that was not his purpose. But for the moment, we will look at some of the "hints" Lewis himself has given us, in the stories and elsewhere, concerning Aslan's "model." As we discuss the various Biblical concepts that Lewis's books echo, our effort will be to show how they may remind us of these ideas or help us understand, perhaps through a simple illustration, what the Bible means. In no way are the Narnia events exact Biblical parallels. But perhaps through seeing Aslan, evil, and many Christian virtues in another world, we may relate them better to our own.

As will be discussed later, the events in *The Lion, the Witch and the Wardrobe* remind us of several events in Christ's own life. And in *The Voyage of the "Dawn Treader,"* when the children reach the End of the World, they see a Lamb who invites them to a breakfast of fish; he is so white they can barely look at him. Suddenly, he is changed, and they recognize him: "As he spoke his snowy white flushed into tawny gold and his size changed and he was Aslan himself, towering above them and scattering, light from his mane."

Similar "symbolism" is used in Revelation 5:5-6:

> The Lion of the Tribe of Judah, the Root of David, has conquered, so that he can open the scroll and its seven seals. And between the throne and the four living creatures and among the elders, I saw a Lamb standing, as though it had been slain.

Aslan also calls himself the great "Bridge Builder" who promises to guide them into Narnia from their world— another Biblical image, as we will see later. Finally, in *The*

Last Battle, Aslan looks to them "no longer as a Lion," and we assume he has taken his human form as he begins to tell them the Great Story, forever and ever.

Elsewhere, Lewis makes it clear that Aslan is a divine figure and that anything "approaching Disney-like humor" would be blasphemy. He wrote the following explanation to a little girl from Texas:

> As to Aslan's other name, well, I want you to guess. Has there never been anyone in this world who (1) Arrived the same time as Father Christmas (2) Said he was the Son of the Great Emperor (3) Gave himself up for someone else's fault to be jeered at and killed by wicked people (4) Came to life again (5) Is sometimes spoken of as a Lamb (at the end of the "Dawn Treader")? Don't you really know His name in this world? (*Letters to Children* 32)

Children who wrote to him knew who Aslan really was, whereas most adults never saw the Biblical connection. In several of his letters, Lewis indicates that he had received many "lovely, moving letters" from children, primarily if brought up in Christian homes, who never failed to grasp the theology of Narnia "more or less unconsciously, and much more clearly than some grownups." Most grown-ups never see who Aslan is, he said. He says he is thankful one girl recognized the  "hidden story" in the Narnia books: "It is odd, children nearly *always* do, grown-ups hardly ever."

A perfect example is a letter written by an 11-year-old girl to Lewis's friend, Owen Barfield:

> I have read Mr. Lewis's books. I got so envoveled [sic] in them all I did was eat, sleep, and read. I wanted to write to you and tell you I understand the books. I mean about the sy[m]bols and all. . . . I know that to me Aslan is God. And all the son's and daughter's of Adam and Eve are God's children. I have my own philosophies

about the books. If it is possible I would like to meet you. None of my friends (well some of them) liked the books. I tried to explain to them but they don't understand about symbols. I never really did until I read the books. (Hooper, "Narnia" 105-6)

In fact, some children understood Aslan so well that they began to love Aslan more than Jesus. Here is Lewis's response to a worried mother of one little boy:

Laurence can't really love Aslan more than Jesus, even if he feels that's what he is doing. For the things he loves Aslan for doing or saying are simply the things Jesus really did and said. So that when Laurence thinks he is loving Aslan, he is really loving Jesus: and perhaps loving Him more than he ever did before. Of course there is one thing Aslan has that Jesus has not—I mean, the body of a lion. (But remember, if there are other worlds and they need to be saved and Christ were to save them—as He would—He may really have taken all sorts of bodies in them which we don't know about). Now if Laurence is bothered because he finds the lion-body seems nicer to him than the man-body, I don't think he need be bothered at all. (*Letters to Children* 52-3).

Why would Lewis choose, as he suggests, to portray Christ as a Lion? First, we must remember that Lewis did not begin writing his stories with Aslan in mind. Instead, he says he had been having dreams of lions at the time, and suddenly Aslan came bounding into the story and "pulled the whole story together and soon He pulled the six other Narnian stories in after Him" (*On Stories* 53). Lewis says he found the name "Aslan" in the Arabian Nights. It is Turkish for Lion and pronounced "Ass-lan." He also says he meant the Lion of Judah (*Letters to Children* 29). Lewis notes that Aslan was always a lion and thus differs from Christ who is God who became man.

Brightness and Fragrance

Lewis associates Aslan with two symbols he said he borrowed from the Grail legend: brightness and a sweet smell. Eustace, for example, notices that although there was no moon when he encountered Aslan, moonlight shone where the Lion was. Shasta, too, sees a whiteness and golden light actually coming from Aslan himself. The light radiating from Aslan is more terrible and more beautiful than anything anyone has ever seen and too bright to look at.

In many of his other works, Lewis associates God and heaven with the Biblical metaphor of light (1 John 1:5, 1 Timothy 6:16), especially in his story "The Man Born Blind." Appropriately, as the children approach Aslan's country at the end of *The Voyage of the "Dawn Treader,"* they notice a "whiteness, shot with faintest colour of gold" spreading around, a "brightness you or I could not bear even if we had dark glasses on." Aslan's brightness contrasts with the dull red light of Jadis' Charn or the sick greenish light of the Shallow-Lands.

Similarly, Aslan's mane gives off a lovely perfume, which contrasts with the foul stench of Tashbaan and its god. Sensing Aslan's warm breath, Shasta knows the "thing" walking beside him is alive. Falling at his feet, he experiences all the glory of his power, his fiery brightness and perfume: "The High King above all kings stooped towards him. Its mane, and some strange and solemn perfume that hung about the mane, was all round him."

A Terrible Good

Aslan manifests a variety of qualities—he is awesome, solemn and stern, yet compassionate and joyful. He both growls and purrs. This paradox of being at the same time both "terrible" and "good" is a key idea in Charles

Williams' *Descent into Hell*, where "terrible" means "full of terror": Pauline "had never considered good as a thing of terror, and certainly she had not supposed a certain thing of terror in her own secret life as any possible good. . . . Salvation. . . . is often a terrible thing—a frightening good." Lewis believed God and the numinous overwhelm us with a sense of dread and awe.

He explains this aspect of Aslan in *The Lion*: "People who have not been in Narnia sometimes think that a thing cannot be good and terrible at the same time." When the children try to look in Aslan's face, they glimpse the "golden mane and the great, royal, solemn, overwhelming eyes; and then they found they couldn't look at him and went all trembly." Digory finds Aslan simultaneously "bigger and more beautiful and more brightly golden and more terrible than he had thought," and Emeth notes that Aslan was "more terrible than the Flaming Mountain of Lagour, and in beauty he surpassed all that is in the world." His speed, says Emeth, is like that of an ostrich, his size like an elephant's, his hair like pure gold, his bright eyes like liquid gold.

Jill senses the same paradoxical combination of terror and moral glory in her first encounter with Aslan at the beginning of *The Silver Chair*. Desperately thirsty, yet paralyzed with fright at the Lion's presence beside the stream, she pleads with him for a promise that he will not harm her. But he will make no such promise, majestically telling her that he has, in fact, "swallowed up girls and boys, women and men, kings and emperors, cities and realms." When Jill reluctantly decides to search for another stream to drink from, Aslan informs her that there is no other. She thus kneels down and begins scooping up water. At first she intends to dash away from the Lion but realizes "that this would be. . . .the most dangerous thing of all."

As all the old tales of Narnia indicate, Aslan is wild—"not a *tame* lion." " 'Ooh!' said Susan, 'I'd thought he was a man. Is he—quite safe? I shall feel rather nervous about meeting a lion.'" Mrs. Beaver replies, "If there's anyone who can appear before Aslan without their knees knocking, they're either braver than most or else just silly." After his resurrection, defying death and evil, Aslan opens his mouth to roar, and "his face became so terrible that they did not dare to look at it. And they saw all the trees in front of him bend before the blast of his roaring."

> "Aslan leaped again . . .whether it was more like playing with a thunderstorm or playing with a kitten Lucy could never make up her mind. . . . the girls no longer felt in the least tired or hungry or thirsty."
> *The Lion, the Witch and the Wardrobe*

Aslan resembles the "devouring" god of the mountain that Lewis portrays in *Till We Have Faces*. But when he hurts, it is for a purpose. First snapping at Hwin to make the horses hurry, the Lion then scratches Aravis. The scratches, he explains later, are equal to the stripes her stepmother whipped into a slave because of her: "You needed to know what it felt like."

Yet Aslan has another side. He can feel all the pain and sorrow of every individual. When Digory fearfully asks Aslan to cure his mother and peers up at his face, what he sees surprises him. Such big, bright, shining tears stand in the Lion's eyes "that for a moment he felt as if the Lion must really be sorrier about his Mother than he was himself." Later, although Digory forgets to say "thank you," Aslan understands without a word from him. Likewise, during Caspian's funeral, Aslan cries great Lion-tears, "each tear more precious than the Earth would be if it was a single solid diamond." He feels great sadness over Edmund's treachery, too.

He can also be joyously playful. Who can forget the lively romp with Aslan that Lucy and Susan experience after his "resurrection"? It is like playing both with a thunderstorm and a kitten. He gives them a wonderful ride on his back. With his mane flying, he never tires, never misses his footing. At the end of *Prince Caspian's* adventures, Aslan leads the children, animals, new followers, and even Bacchus himself in a riotous, festive parade through town. He playfully tosses the disbelieving Trumpkin in the air, then asks to be his friend.

A Guide in Other Forms

As a Lion, Aslan can show us the full significance of the incarnation—Christ becoming a man, like us. This concept is exemplified in *The Lion* when Aslan tells the other lions to join with him in battle. One lion replies, "Did you hear what he said? Us lions. That means him and me. Us lions."

We cannot read very many pages of a Narnia story without sensing Aslan's presence, though unseen and often in another form, and guidance of events. Like God, he is wise and foreknowing. As Puddleglum reminds the children, there are no accidents: "He was there when the giant king caused the letters to be cut, and he knew already all things that would come of them; including this." Tirian describes whatever may befall them in the future as "the adventure that Aslan would send them."

In *The Voyage of the "Dawn Treader,"* Aslan appears as an albatross, deliciously breathing "Courage, dear heart," to Lucy, then guiding them away from the Dark

Island. Throughout all of Shasta's adventures—the lions forcing him to protect Aravis and snapping at the horses; the Cat protecting him at the tombs; the unseen giant shadow keeping to his left to protect him from the cliff; even his own coming to Calormen—it is Aslan who guides each step of the way. "You may call me a giant," he tells Shasta; "Tell me your sorrows." Then he reveals to him that he is the One Lion who has been with him all along. Shasta later realizes it isn't "luck" that sent him through the pass in the mountains into Narnia "but Him." Aravis, too, at first thinking it "luck" that the lion only gave her ten scratches, is told by the Hermit that in his 109 years, he "never yet met any such thing as Luck."

Aslan is ever present to warn the children sternly from time to time not to do wrong. He reproves not out of anger but because he always knows what is best for them. Usually, Aslan's growling face is all the children need to remind them of their wrongdoing and responsibility or make them confess their real motives. Some day, in Aslan's country, they will never do the wrong things and then "I will not always be scolding," he promises. When they bicker about the gold on Deathwater Island, suddenly Aslan's growling face appears to remind them of their wrongdoing. Just as Lucy begins to say the spell in the Magician's Book to make herself beautiful, Aslan stares gravely at her from the page. In *Prince Caspian* a stern look from Aslan is all she needs to tell her that it is truly her responsibility to follow him, despite the others. As the Lion looks into her eyes, Lucy begins to argue that she couldn't have left the others to come up to him alone: "Don't look at me like that. . . .oh well, I suppose I *could*."

One cannot help but tell the truth before Aslan's holy stare. Digory is forced to confess fully to Aslan his responsibility for the Witch entering Narnia: "'She woke up,' said Digory wretchedly. And then, turning very white,

'I mean, I woke her.'" Jill, too, confesses that she shoved
Eustace over the cliff simply because she was showing
off. Later, Aslan must appear to her in a dream to remind
her to repeat the Signs and give her a clue: UNDER ME.
Finally, just as Moses is permitted to see only God's back
and not his face because his glory is too great (Exodus
33:21-23), Aslan wreaks his fury upon Experiment
House, permitting the hysterical teacher and students to
see only his back.

The power of Aslan's wonderfully warm, sweet breath,
and the air from his tossing mane, give such power and
peace that it often seems reminiscent of the power and
guidance of the Holy Spirit. The whole trinity is perhaps
hinted at when Shasta asks the "ghostly" companion
walking beside him, "Who are you?" " 'Myself' said the
Voice, very deep and low so that the earth shook, and
again 'Myself,' loud and clear and gay, and then the third
time 'Myself,' whispered so softly you could hardly hear
it." Aslan has guided him all along.

Aslan's breath and kiss always empower the children.
When he sends Digory to get the apple seed, Digory
doesn't know *how* he will do it. But Aslan's kiss gives him
such new strength and courage that he feels sure that
he can do it. When Lucy buries her face in his mane, it
makes her a disciple, for he breathes such lion strength
into her that he declares her a "lioness." He breathes on
Edmund so that a greatness hangs all about him, too. To
wake the statues in *The Lion,* he breathes on their frozen
forms, imparting renewed life to them. Similarly, he
breathes on the chosen Talking Animals when Narnia is
created to separate them from the others.

Because of this Divine Plan and Presence behind
events, we are to have faith in Aslan even when we cannot
see or know and to be content with the present. The
Green Lady in *Perelandra* believes that the wave sent to

her from God at each moment is the best wave of all. So too, Aslan repeatedly tells the children, "Did I not explain to you once before that no one is ever told what *would have happened?*" That is not to say that Aslan dictates every event that happens or will always be present even if not asked. In fact, Lewis clearly illustrates the importance of free will and prayer in our lives. Aslan does not appear as a guide and comfort in the form of an albatross until Lucy whispers, "Aslan, Aslan, Aslan, if ever you loved us at all, send us help now." Even though the darkness seems to remain, she *feels* better because of her small faith until he comes.

Likewise, in *The Last Battle*, Tirian cries out "Aslan! Aslan! Aslan! Come and help us Now." For him, too, the darkness, cold and quiet seem just the same, but there is a kind of change inside him: "Without knowing why, he began to feel a faint hope. And he felt somehow stronger." And help does come. Although no one can successfully *try* to get to Narnia, in *The Silver Chair,* Jill and Eustace enter not long after they plead with Aslan to let them in: "Aslan, Aslan, Aslan! . . . Please let us two go into—." We sense that Aslan, like God, wants us to call on him first. Wondering if Aslan knows how hungry they are without telling him, Digory and Polly must have Fledge the horse explain it to them: "I've no doubt he would," says Fledge. "But I've a sort of idea he likes to be asked."

Reactions to Aslan

An individual's reaction to Aslan reveals what kind of person he is. A curious thing happens, for example, when all four Pevensies hear the word "Aslan" spoken for the first time. At the sound of his name, each child feels quite different. Lewis likens it to the contrast between a terrifying or wonderful reaction to one dream: "At the name of Aslan each one of the children felt something jump inside." Edmund feels a sense of mysterious horror and, he later admits, hates the name. Peter feels brave and adventurous. Susan feels like a delicious smell or a delightful stream of music has floated by. And Lucy gets the "feeling you have when you wake up in the morning and realize that it is the beginning of the holidays or the beginning of summer."

There are similar varied reactions to Aslan's song of creation. The Cabby, Digory, and Polly drink in the music, for it reminds them of something. The Witch, on the other hand, knows what the song is and hates it. Andrew doesn't like it because it makes him think and feel things he doesn't want to. He tells himself it is "only a lion" who hasn't really been singing—only roaring. And soon "he couldn't have heard anything else even if he had wanted to." Aslan explains that Andrew has made himself unable to hear his voice: "If I spoke to him, he would hear only growlings and roarings. Oh Adam's sons, how cleverly you defend yourself against all that might do you good!" Just the sight of Aslan creates "one single expression of terror" on the mean, cruel faces of the Experiment House children. A person's attitude also affects his view of Narnia itself—Andrew, Eustace and the Telmarines all dread the thought of going there.

Thus "what you see and hear depends a good deal on where you are standing: it also depends on what sort of person you are." The dwarfs refuse to believe in Aslan even when presented with the truth from Tirian. Like Andrew, they sit huddled up in the Stable and see only darkness instead of the sky and flowers that the children find in the same place. To the dwarfs, the flowers smell like stable litter. They can't even distinguish Aslan's voice. And his glorious feast—pies, tongues, pigeons, trifles, ices, and wine—tastes only like old turnips, raw cabbage leaves, and dirty trough water. Andrew and these dwarfs are much like Orual in *Till We Have Faces,* who believes the wine and bread Psyche gives her are just water and berries. Aslan explains that a person can close his own eyes to the truth: "They have chosen cunning instead of belief. Their prison is only in their own minds."

One reason for the tendency to lose faith in Aslan is that he is not always in Narnia but comes and goes. Caspian, for example, who has never seen Aslan or Talking Beasts, begins to wonder if they are only stories after all. Nikabrik actually calls on the power of the Witch rather than Aslan because he has heard so little about him. After Aslan's resurrection, "he just fades out of the story," Nikabrik argues. "How do you explain that, if he really came to life? Isn't it much more likely that he didn't, and that the stories say nothing more about him because there was nothing more to say?" How similar this is to many of the arguments we hear about Christ. Even Peter argues that if Narnia or anything else is real, then they are here all the time. "Are they?" asks Professor Kirke, hinting at the necessity for faith instead of sight.

In *Prince Caspian,* the children's faith determines when and how they see Aslan during their journey to Aslan's How. Lucy, who loves Aslan perhaps more than anyone, sees him first. The voice she likes best in the world commands, "Follow me." Although the others don't believe and grumble loudly, they follow her nevertheless. Certainly they won't see him at first, Aslan predicts. "Later on, it depends." Edmund, who after all his misfortunes in an earlier adventure has learned his lesson, sees the Shadow next; then Peter, and finally, Susan and Trumpkin. Susan admits that her own attitude kept her from seeing him: "I really believed it was him tonight when you woke us up. I mean, deep down inside. Or I could have, if I'd let myself." How much she is like Edmund, who deep down inside had also known that the White Witch was bad.

One's response to Aslan is actually indicative of both his relationship to the Lion and his faith. Spiritual growth permits an even clearer vision of him. "Aslan," says Lucy, "You're bigger." "Every year you grow, you will find me bigger," Aslan explains. When she thumbs through the Magician's Book, then gazes up from the picture, she sees Aslan. "I have been here all the time," said he, "but you have just made me visible." One's response to Aslan also reflects his unique relationship to God. Aslan tells Shasta and Aravis on separate occasions that "No one is told any story but their own."

Faith in Aslan must also come from the heart. Emeth is accepted into Aslan's country because his motives are true: "Son, thou art welcome. . . . All the service thou hast done to Tash, I account as service done to me." In contrast, Susan apparently never really believes in her heart, for she is not granted final admission to Aslan's country. Bree, like Thomas in the Bible, refuses to believe Aslan is a real lion and must receive proof before he will believe. Just as Christ urged Thomas to put his fingers in the nail prints in his hands and feet, Aslan bids Bree: "Touch me. Smell me. Here are my paws, here is my tail, these are my whiskers. I am a true Beast." When disbelieving and stubborn Trumpkin doesn't believe Aslan is a real Lion either, Aslan proves his reality merely by tossing him gently into the air.

Time and time again, the children are called to simply have faith in Aslan. When the leopards are afraid to go near the Witch for fear she will turn them into stone, Peter tells Lucy to simply trust Aslan: "It'll be all right. . . . He wouldn't send them if it weren't." As Ramandu's daughter tells Caspian's group, "You can't know. . . .

You can only believe—or not." Who best illustrates this but Puddleglum, who tells the Green Witch that even if the world of trees, grass, sun, moon, stars—even Aslan himself—is made up, "the made-up things seem a good deal more important than the real ones. . . . I'm going to stand by the play world." How wonderful that not only is his faith grounded in a solid reality but in a more perfect reality than he has ever dreamed of.

In *The Lion*, the children fail to believe in Lucy's story about Narnia. The professor uses the following logic. There are only three possibilities: Lucy is telling lies, is mad, or is telling the truth. Because she never lies and is not mad, they must assume that she is telling the truth. Lewis uses the same sort of argument in *Mere Christianity* concerning belief in the claims Christ made about himself: either he was a lunatic, or a devil of hell—or the Son of God himself.

All these varied reactions to Aslan—hate, belief, belief only with proof—parallel one's reaction to the White Witch, so that a person's attitude toward her similarly reflects his spiritual "guard." Polly immediately dislikes her, just as Aunt Letty, totally unimpressed, calls her a "shameless hussy." In contrast, both Digory and Andrew are awed by her beauty.

No matter which "side" one is on, once one has been in the presence of either Aslan or the Witch, his perspective is never the same. After seeing the Witch, the children find Andrew much less fearsome; after being in the Magic Wood, the tunnel above their house seems drab and homely. The Apple of Life makes everything in London pale in comparison: "All those other things seemed to have scarcely any colour at all. Every one of them, even the sunlight, looked faded and dingy. . . . Nothing else was worth looking at: indeed you couldn't look at anything else."

Certainly, after meeting Aslan the Lion and being in his secret country—no matter what your reaction—you are never the same.

Creation

Who can forget the image in *The Magician's Nephew* of Aslan singing Narnia into existence—to see that Singer makes the viewer forget everything else: "It was a Lion. Huge, shaggy, and bright it stood facing the risen sun. Its mouth was wide open in song." The experience of his presence is like "a sea of tossing gold in which they were floating, and such a sweetness and power rolled about them and over them and entered into them that they felt they had never really been happy or wise or good, or ever alive and awake, before." The memory of this "golden goodness" remains with them their whole lives, reassuring them in times of need that all is well. Aslan is the first thing the animals see when they are created. Even the trees bow down to him.

In Genesis, God created the world by his *Word*: first, the heaven and earth—once a shapeless, chaotic void—then light, sky and water, dry land; grass, plants and trees; sun and moon; sea creatures and birds; wild animals and reptiles; and at last, man. Aslan also creates Narnia from an empty world—"Nothing." It is dark and cold, but there is cool, flat earthy substance underfoot. Then Aslan sings the world into creation: first the stars, planets and sun; then rivers, valleys, hills, rocks and water; grass and vegetation; trees; and finally, animals and insects. God's commands of "Let there be" are echoed by Aslan's "Be walking trees. Be talking beasts. Be divine waters." Fledge also echoes the Genesis chapters when Aslan asks him about his flying: "It is good. . . . It is very good."

The human kings and queens of Narnia are entreated to rule the creatures kindly and fairly because all Narnians are free subjects. Aslan chooses two of each animal and touches their noses with his. This, of course, reminds us of Noah in Genesis 6:19 choosing two of each animal, who are to multiply and inhabit the world after the Flood. With  Aslan's breath comes a flash like fire upon the chosen animals. This image seems to be used throughout the Narnia tales as a signal of the Holy Spirit, or of Aslan's empowering of his followers. His warning to them is like that which God makes to man: "Creatures, I give you yourselves. . . . I give to you forever this land of Narnia." He warns them to treat the Dumb Beasts gently and to cherish them but to not "go back to their ways lest you cease to be Talking Beasts. For out of them you were taken and into them you can return." Adam and Eve are told that all the earth is to be subdued under them. But in Genesis 3:19 after their Fall, God tells them that as they were made from the ground, to the ground they will return.

The Tree and Garden

Although man himself is not created in Narnia, he plays an important role there. As on earth, man is directly responsible for the entrance of evil into the new world: "You come of the Lord Adam and the Lady Eve," says Aslan. "And that is both honour enough to erect the head of the poorest beggar, and shame enough to bow the shoulders of the greatest emperor in earth."

Digory, for instance, is directly responsible for awakening Jadis because of his uncontrollable curiosity to know what will happen if he hits the bell. When Digory succumbs to the temptation, he awakens the Witch. Lewis deals with temptation in many of his novels, especially *Perelandra*, and it occurs in various guises in the Narnia books as well. Temptation is frequently experienced in the desire to know. Appropriately, Jadis enters Narnia before it is even five hours old by Digory's grabbing onto her heel. She kicks him with her heel and cuts him in the mouth. This detail is reminiscent of God's punishment of Satan and Eve: "He shall strike you on your head, while you will strike at his heel" (Gen. 3:15). Just as Adam and Eve are told that they must struggle to extract a living from the soil, Aslan asks King Frank if he can use a spade and plough and raise food from the ground.

Later, Aslan sends Digory on a special mission: to bring back one of its silver-gold apples, with seeds to plant in the newly-created Narnia. He is told to go to the Western Wilds, where he will find a green hill at the end of a lake. On top is a garden with a tree at its center. The apples of this tree cast a light of their own. Roosting in its branches is a bird, larger than an eagle, with saffron breast, head crested with scarlet, and purple tail. Like Aslan himself, this garden is permeated with a warm, sweet, golden smell that brings tears to Digory's eyes. The hill itself is surrounded by a high wall of green turf and trees of blue and silver.

Facing east—toward Aslan's country—are the golden gates that say:

Come in by the gold gates or not at all,
Take of my fruit for others or forbear.
For those who steal or those who climb my wall
Shall find their heart's desire and find despair.

Central within the garden is a tree of life. Such hunger
and thirst overcome Digory that he longs just to taste the
fruit. He sees the Witch eating an apple but notices that
it makes a horrid red stain on her mouth. If he doesn't
listen to her, she warns, he will miss some "knowledge
that would have made you happy all your life": "It is the
apple of youth, the apple of life. . . . Eat it, Boy, eat it; and
You and I will both live forever and be king and queen of
this whole world."

Although this appeal certainly is tempting, an even
greater temptation for Digory is Jadis's suggestion that
he take an apple to save his mother before completing
his task for Aslan. She assures him that his home will
once again be happy, and he will be like other boys. "Oh!"
Digory gasps as if hurt, and he puts his hand to his head.
Digory now realizes the "terrible choice" that lies before
him. The Witch urges him to follow her suggestion by
reasoning that the Lion hasn't done anything that would
make Digory his slave and can't help him in this world
anyway. Besides, what would his mother think? Such a
wild animal must have made him cruel to make such silly
promises. Polly, in fact, could stay here, so no one would
need to know. This last suggestion is so patently mean
that Digory realizes the falsehood and hollowness of the
Witch's "logic."

As a result of her eating of the fruit, all apples become
a horror to Jadis. Aslan explains that this will happen to
all those who pluck and eat fruits at the wrong time and
in the wrong way—those who disobey him and satisfy
their own prideful lust for power: "The fruit is good, but
they loathe it ever after." True, Jadis is granted her desire

for strength and endless days, but she receives eternal misery as well. Thus Uncle Andrew's "prophecy" that "no great wisdom can be reached without sacrifice" comes true.

Unlike Adam and Eve, Digory does not succumb to the temptation to eat the fruit. Instead, he takes the apple straight to Aslan. Because Digory has "hungered and thirsted and wept" for this fruit, he is permitted to sow the seed in Narnia himself by simply tossing it into soft soil. The tree that grows protects Narnia from the Witch for many years. It grows quickly, casting a light from its apples of silver and sending forth a breath-taking smell. Like the Tree in Eden, the fruit of this tree can bring joy, healing, and protection when used in the right way, but death and horror and despair when taken in selfish disobedience. For example, it is called the "Apple of Life" for Digory's mother because it is eaten in the right way and time. But it gives an endless life of misery to the Witch because she plucked the apple in her own way, for herself.

God planted the Tree of Life and the Tree of the Knowledge of Good and Evil in the Garden of Eden. But because man disobeyed and ate of the second tree, God punished him, separating him from both trees (Genesis 2:17, 3:24). Some day, however, believers will be restored to partake of the Tree of Life (Revelation 22:2) because of Christ's sacrifice on a tree on a hill.

Besides the tree of protection, three other trees grow in Narnia: a toffee tree (from Polly's candy) and a gold and a silver tree (from coins that fall from Andrew's pockets). Similarly, a complete lamp-post grows from just the cross-bar of a lamp-post from London. These all illustrate the miracle of growth to be found in Narnia, as well as the temptation to capitalize on it.

Evil

Besides the temptation in the garden, the Narnia tales are filled with conflict against evil forces that attempt to dominate individuals' wills and lives. Lewis makes it plain that evil must be fought within two levels: as both a spiritual and physical warfare.

Temptation

In *The Lion, the Witch and the Wardrobe*, greed is vividly portrayed when the Witch tempts Edmund with Turkish Delight. This is a candy that makes you want it more than anything else, so that you would eat it till you kill yourself.

Edmund's greed also appears in his desire to be King, as the Witch promises, and to have all his brothers and sisters under him. Of course, the Witch tosses in a few other ploys as well: she enlarges upon his handsomeness and tricks him into not telling the others about her.

Food becomes the main bait in *The Silver Chair* when the children's obsession for the giant's food, as promised by the Green Witch, distracts them from looking for Aslan's Signs. Gold and riches are also common objects of temptation. On Deathwater Island, lust for gold makes

---

TURKISH DELIGHT

Ingredients:
- 2 cups granulated sugar
- 1 $\frac{1}{4}$ cups water
- 1 lemon
- 1 orange
- 4 tablespoons unflavored powdered gelatin
- 2 tablespoons confectioners' sugar
- 1 tablespoon cornstarch

Steps:
1. Dissolve the granulated sugar in half of the water over medium heat.
2. Cut the lemon and orange peels into strips, and squeeze and strain the juices. Add both.
3. Bring the mixture to a boil.
4. Simmer for 15 minutes.
5. Soak the gelatin in the mixture for 5 to 10 minutes.
6. Strain the mixture into a shallow, dampened pan or onto platters.
7. Let it set for 24 hours.
8. Cut the candy into 1-inch squares.
9. Sift the confectioners's sugar and cornstarch together into a shallow dish.
10. Roll the pieces of candy in the mixture.
11. Store the squares in boxes with more confectioners' sugar and cornstarch between each layer.

---

the children so greedily quarrelsome that only a stern glare from Aslan reminds them that they have sinned. And what better image of greed can we discover than Eustace sleeping on the dragon's treasure, his pockets bursting with jewels. Filled with dragonish thoughts, Eustace turns into a dragon.

Lucy undergoes two different temptations as she reads the Magician's Magic Book. First, she discovers a spell to make her beautiful beyond the lot of mortals. She sees herself throned and lovely, with all the kings fighting for her so that even her sister Susan is jealous. But Lucy has the feeling she mustn't succumb to this temptation, and a growl from Aslan confirms her intuition. But she does give in to the temptation to have the forbidden knowledge of knowing what her friends think about her, perhaps spoiling the potential for lifelong friendships.

Pride is the root problem of most who are sucked in by temptation or are evil themselves. Jadis boasts of her power as ruler of Charn and her possession of the Deplorable Word: "Ours is a high and lonely destiny." As Queen of Charn, Jadis believes her people exist only to do her will. Digory notes that she never seems interested in objects or people unless she can use them, concentrating her attention on those she needs at the moment. In *The Last Battle,* Shift, who defines "true freedom" as "doing what I tell you," echoes this attitude.

Uncle Andrew, though certainly a feeble parallel to Jadis, is much like her. He is greedy for wisdom and for power. Dabbling in magic in order to discover new, unseen worlds, he tricks the children into doing his dirty work for him. He is vain enough to think that he called Jadis to England and even deludes himself that she is beginning to love him. Once he gets into Narnia himself, he worries about his own fate: "What about me? They don't seem to think of that. No one thinks of me." He also tries to capitalize on Narnia's ability to grow gold and silver trees from coins.

Andrew speaks Jadis's very words: "Men like me who possess hidden wisdom are freed from common rules just as we are cut off from common pleasures. Ours, my boy, is a high and lonely destiny." Digory perceptively realizes that what Andrew really means is that he can do anything he likes to get anything he wants. The Witch, Andrew, and their like have no rules. How unlike Aslan, who obeys even his own rules.

Caspian, though not as self-centered as these two, slips into selfishness when he longs to abandon his ship and country and sail on to the End of the World. Reepicheep sternly warns him not to please himself with adventures as if he were a private person. This is a hard lesson, learned over and over again by the children and other Narnians. They must obey first and help others, not themselves.

Digory, for instance, must get the apple seed before Aslan will help his mother; and surprisingly, when he does succeed in his task, he feels no conceit at all. After his long bout with the Witch, Edmund, too, finally stops thinking about himself: "He just went on looking at Aslan." Even Bree, who perpetually worries about his looks and social respectability, must learn that he won't be anyone special in Narnia; through Aslan he loses his self-conceit. As Aslan teaches, if you feel yourself self-sufficient, it is proof that you are not.

Effects of Evil

Other effects of evil can readily be seen. An obvious example is the comparison of the worlds of Aslan and the mock worlds conceived by evil: Charn and the Shallow-

Lands. These are nothing but dead worlds. The Witch turns even Narnia into an icy white enchantment where the frozen animal "statues" seem to reflect nature's retreat as a consequence of evil. In *The Last Battle*, deception results in cutting down trees and silencing and harnessing talking horses. There is the same kind of slavery, sadness, fear and gloom that can be found in the Shallow-Lands.

Evil also sets out to corrupt the truths about reality and makes us forget the glimpses and glimmers of the "numinous" that appear to us all through our lives. Jadis has no recollection of ever having been in the quiet place of the magic Wood Between the Worlds. The Green Witch claims that her lamp is real and the sun a fake. And under the enchantment of the Green Witch, Rilian says he cannot even remember his true self. But evil never totally conquers. Rilian is allowed to be himself one hour a day.

Telmarines like Miraz call all stories about Narnia and Aslan "old wives' fables" and silly lies. Nikabrik similarly doubts the stories and wants to call on the power of the White Witch. These examples illustrate what can happen when our experiences of God and heaven become further and further removed from the experiences of the ancient Biblical writers. We begin to view what they say as simply metaphors rather than solid facts.

Evil tries to set up false gods. Shift creates a parody of Aslan and tries to make the creatures believe that Aslan is not the one they have longed for and believed in. These Narnians actually begin to doubt their belief altogether, thinking the changes in Narnia are punishment for a terrible wrong. Next, Shift's group tries to confuse Aslan and Tash by merging them into Tashlan. The god Tash (whose name appropriately means "blemish") is the Calormene god who requires human sacrifices. Its birdlike head has a "cruel, curved beak." The four arms it holds above its head stretch north as if "it wanted to snatch all Narnia in its grip." Twenty curved fingers have long, pointed, bird-like claws. How different is its deathly smell from the fragrant breath of Aslan. As Shift and the others begin to equate Tash and Aslan, the Narnians wonder how a god who feeds on blood could be the same as the good Lion by whose blood all Narnia was saved.

A result of the false Aslan is that people stop believing in the real Aslan. Even worse, perhaps, is the "enlightened" philosophy of Ginger the Cat, who is cockily convinced that neither god exists. Sadly for him, he discovers that Tash does exist. Lewis vividly shows the reality of demons. When the Unicorn acknowledges that "there is a real Tash, after all," the Dwarf replies that the foolish Ape will get more than he bargained for: "He called for Tash: Tash has come." Because Rabadash similarly calls on Tash, Aslan allows him to be a man in Tash's temple but a donkey if he leaves.

Edmund is a prime case study in the gradual effects of sin. After he returns home from Narnia, he first lies about having been there. Then his behavior becomes nastier and nastier as the sin eats away at him. Feeling snubbed, he increasingly resents his brother and wants to get even with him. The Beavers note the evil look in his eyes, the "horrible ideas" in his head. Worst of all, he mocks Aslan, painting an impertinent moustache on a lion statue.

Problems in Discerning Evil

No matter how obvious its effects, evil is not always easily detected. Edmund defines well the problem of perceiving and understanding evil: "Which is the right side? How do we know the fauns are in the right and the Queen. . . is in the wrong. We don't really know anything

about either." "How do we know?" he queries. Part of
the White Witch's magic, says Lewis, is that she can
make things appear to be what they aren't. She certainly
doesn't look like our usual conception of the Devil. The
Green Witch, too, is disguised as a beautiful woman
in a green garment. With her lovely voice, she not only
deceives Rilian into believing she is all good, but the
children also fail to recognize her as the green serpent.

In *The Last Battle*, Shift uses both false appearances
with the lion's skin and also a deceptive logic and a
cunning twisting of the facts. He misinterprets every one
of the signs for Puzzle, then tricks poor Puzzle into doing
what he wants.

In *Prince Caspian*, Lucy hypothesizes about the
deceptiveness of evil that may come to our world. How
dreadful it would be if "men started going wild inside, like
the animals here, and still looked like men, so that you'd
never know which were which."

So how do we perceive evil? Quite often in the tales,
the children are told they can recognize friends who have
been in Narnia, or evil people, simply "by their eyes." At
Aslan's Table, when Edmund is skeptical about whether
or not Ramandu's daughter can be trusted and the food
is safe to eat, she says, "You can't know. . . . You can only
believe or not." But more often, we may really find the
answer deep within us. Down deep inside, for example,
Edmund says he knew that the Witch was really bad and
cruel. As we have seen, one's response to a witch or to
Aslan reflects the kind of person he or she really is.

Sacrifice and Resurrection

Just as humans brings evil into Narnia, they will help
restore it. But Aslan says, " I will see to it that the worst
falls upon myself. . . . As Adam's race has done the harm,

Adam's race shall help heal it." Is this not like Christ's cure for sin through becoming a man himself? "Death came into the world because of what man (Adam) did, and it is because of what this other man (Christ) has done that now there is the resurrection from the dead" (1 Corinthians 15:21).

The events of *The Lion, the Witch and the Wardrobe* remind us in many ways of Christ's crucifixion and resurrection, but they in no way exactly parallel the account in the Bible. They do, however, give us a new understanding of atonement and rebirth in Christ.

According to Narnian history, the Emperor-Over-Sea sent a Deep Magic into the world from the "Dawn of Time." This Magic permits the Witch to kill every traitor, and unless she has blood, Narnia will perish in water and fire. This Law is written three places:

(1) the Stone Table
(2) the Trunk of the World Ash Tree
(3) the Emperor's sceptre

It is similar to God's Old Testament Law that is written on the stone tablets, requiring death and the shedding of blood as the penalty for sin. Quite simply, it is the moral law that demands justice for evil.

But further back in time is a Deeper Magic about which the Witch knows nothing. This Law states that when a willing victim who has committed no treachery is killed in the traitor's stead, the Stone Table will crack, and Death will start working backwards.

What a marvelously succinct expression of the New Testament message of sacrifice for others due to love and grace. According to New Testament "Law," the Law of Love, when Christ is sacrificed as the perfect substitute for man, the Old Testament Law is "cracked"—God's demand is met, paid for, and Death no longer has a hold on us: "For the wages of sin is death, but the free gift of God is eternal life through Jesus Christ our Lord" (Romans 6:23).

Aslan is said to have "saved Narnia." Aslan is sacrificed only for Edmund, though; and this is different from the Biblical idea of one individual's atonement for all mankind. Yet this brings down to earth the very personal sacrifice involved. Christ died, and would have died, even for one individual.

Just as Christ's disciples expected him to help them as their savior who would deliver them from earthly oppression then and there, so too the children talk happily of the future battle and of Aslan's leading them in deliverance from the Witch's forces. "You will be there yourself, Aslan," says Peter. But Aslan promises nothing. He is, in fact, strangely sad and deep in thought, for he knows he must pay the price for the Judas-like traitor, Edmund.

Like Jesus's evening in the Garden of Gethsemane, Aslan's last night is expectant and troubled. Lucy and Susan, like Christ's faithful disciples, follow Aslan into the Great Woods, but "his tail and head hung low and he walked slowly as if he were very, very tired." For perhaps the first time in our lives, we can visualize what it was like for Christ to know he would have to die: "Oh, children, children, children, why are you following me?" Aslan asks. He tells them to promise to stop when he bids them to, so he can go on alone. Until then, they walk with him and comfort him (and themselves) by burying their hands in his mane.

Then they watch him go on quietly and alone to confront the Witch and her band of horrible creatures. Just as Christ was, Aslan is mocked, kicked, hit, spit on, and jeered: "Puss, Puss! Poor Pussy." "How many mice have you caught today, Cat?" But even when muzzled,

Aslan looks beautiful and patient. Just as Christ could have called the angels to rescue him, so too Aslan could have broken out of his bonds if he had wanted to, Lucy observes.

Aslan is not sacrificed on a cross but on a Stone Table located on the middle of an open hilltop in the Great Woods. It is a slab of gray stone supported by other stones, with strange lines and figures inscribed on it. Stabbing him with a stone knife with a "strange and evil shape," the Witch jeers, "You have given me Narnia forever, you have lost your own life and you have not saved his."

In Lewis's book *Till We Have Faces*, he uses the stone as a symbol of an ancient, pagan religion. So he may be using the stone slab, with its strange writing, and the stone knife as symbols for God's law, which requires death as a penalty for sin. When the sacrifice is over, the Table is divided in two, as was the veil in the Tabernacle after Christ's crucifixion.

With Aslan, Christmas comes for the first time in 100 years. The time between his first arrival in Narnia and the coming of spring is appropriately about three months— when Easter occurs. Lucy and Susan remind us of the women who returned dejectedly on Easter morning to Christ's tomb. The girls, who have looked away during the "hopeless and horrid" murder, later return sadly to the scene of dead calm. But gradually, changes begin to happen. The sky slowly lightens; the mice nibble away at the cords that hold Aslan to the table. Then they see Aslan himself—resurrected—more full of life than ever: "It's more magic," they whisper. Looking around, they see Aslan himself, larger than they have ever seen him before, standing in the sunrise and shaking his mane. Is he a ghost? The warm breath and rich smell assure them he is not.

> "Then he caught hold of me. . . and threw me into the water. It smarted like anything but only for a moment. After that it became perfectly delicious and as soon as I started swimming and splashing I found that all the pain had gone from my arm. And then I saw why. I'd turned into a boy again."
>
> *The Voyage of the "Dawn Treader"*

Salvation

While Aslan's sacrifice may not exactly parallel the events of Christ's crucifixion, it does illustrate his personal sacrifice for Edmund's sin. After privately walking and talking with Aslan, Edmund is his real self for the first time in his life. When Lucy and Susan romp with Aslan after his sacrifice, they no longer feel tired, hungry, or thirsty. Lewis uses water as an image of salvation and its regenerating power.

Undragoning

Eustace's is one of the most striking episodes in the Chronicles and a wonderful image of salvation and consequent penetration to the true self. Eustace Clarence Scrubb, the typical stuffed shirt snob, is turned appropriately into a dragon, in whose likeness, through loneliness, he learns about friendship.

But the real change—his undragoning—can only come from Aslan himself. First, he feels Aslan commanding, "Follow me." Then Aslan takes him to a garden with a well at the center. (From the description, we assume he is taken to the mountains of Aslan's country). Next, the

Lion tells him to undress. As Edmund begins scratching, his scales begin falling off. "And then I scratched a little deeper and, instead of just scales coming off here and there, my whole skin started peeling off beautifully, like it does after an illness, or as if I was a banana."

But as he starts going into the well to bathe, he looks down and sees "that it was all hard and rough and wrinkled and scaly just as it had been before. . . . So I scratched and tore again and this underskin peeled off beautifully and out I stepped and left it lying beside the other one." But the exact same thing happens, and he scratches off yet another layer. "You will have to let me undress you," says Aslan.

When Aslan tears off the skin with his claws, it hurts worse than anything Edmund has ever felt, but it feels good to have the ugly, dark, knobbly stuff gone. Aslan then tosses him into the stingingly cold, clear water, and the pain in his arm disappears. He also finds himself somehow dressed in new clothes. "The cure had begun." Everyone notices the change in Eustace's behavior after his undragoning.

This episode is a perfect illustration of what happens when Christ gets hold of a sinner and makes him a new creature. We ourselves are unable to peel away our layers of sin and selfishness; in fact, we find that such ugliness has penetrated to the very roots, the center of our lives. The experience of letting Christ do it for us may hurt, but he bathes us in the water of new life and re-clothes us as new creations. Our behavior cannot help but be changed: "When someone becomes a Christian he becomes a brand new person inside. He is not the same any more. A new life has begun!" (2 Corinthians 5:17).

Water

In another vivid example, Lewis uses the same Biblical symbol of water to show the regenerating power of salvation. When Digory walks into the garden to pick the apple for his mother, a terrible thirst and hunger come over him. In John 4:13-14, Jesus tells a woman, "Every one who drinks of this water will thirst again, but whoever drinks of the water that I shall give him will never thirst; the water that I shall give him will become in him a spring of water welling up to eternal life." Throughout the Bible, living water and the river of living water flowing from the throne of God are used to symbolically describe new life and the blessings flowing from the heart of the believer (Revelation 22:1-2; John 7:37-39).

In *The Silver Chair*, Jill is thirsty but afraid to approach a stream because a great Lion is standing on the other side: "I daren't come and drink," says Jill. "Then you will die of thirst," replies the Lion. "Oh dear!" says Jill coming closer. "I suppose I must go and look for another stream then." "There is no other stream," the Lion answers. So Jill kneels and drinks the coldest and most refreshing water she has ever had, and it quenches her thirst at once.

Similarly, after Shasta meets and communes with Aslan on the mountain-side, he notices the deep, large footprint left in the grass. "As he looked at it, water had already filled the bottom of it. Soon it was full to the brim, and then overflowing, and a little stream was running downhill, past him, over the grass." This little stream provides Shasta with the refreshment he needs.

In *The Last Battle*, Tirian and his band of followers, while hiding near the Stable by a white rock, discover a trickle of water flowing down the rock face into a little pool. Just when they need it most in the heat of battle, they are provided with the most delicious drink they have ever had. While they drink it, they are perfectly happy and cannot think of anything else.

Similarly, when the group sails to the End of the World in *The Voyage of the "Dawn Treader,"* they don't want to eat or sleep. But they draw buckets of dazzling water from the sea that is "stronger than wine and somehow wetter, more liquid, than ordinary water." Some of the older sailors grow younger each day, and everyone is filled with joy.

The idea of spiritual refreshment and reward also seems to be depicted by Aslan's Table, which the children discover during their adventures on the "Dawn Treader." Aslan's How, also called the Hill of the Stone Table, contains a hilltop with the broken Stone Table on it. Surrounding the Table is a mound containing tunnels, ancient writings, and stone reliefs of Aslan. The Stone Knife used to kill Aslan is honored here. Perhaps an image of the Communion table, Aslan's Table is set by Aslan's bidding for those who come that far to the World's End. This sumptuous banquet is more magnificent than the children have ever seen.

Like the manna God provided for the Israelites, the food is "eaten, and renewed, every day," for large white birds carry away all uneaten morsels. Ramandu is brought a small fruit, like a live coal, which is set on his tongue—a fireberry that takes his age away little by little.

Appropriately, Aslan tells the children that the door to Aslan's country is from their own world—across a river. Aslan calls himself the great Bridge Builder. To arrive there, the children scale a Waterfall that leads them to the Golden Gates. In *The Weight of Glory*, Lewis writes, "What would it be to taste at the fountain-head that stream of which even these lower reaches prove so intoxicating? Yet that, I believe, is what lies before us. The whole man is to drink from the fountain of joy" (14). The next chapter describes Lewis's longing for Joy and the children's final adventure through the Stable Door.

Stepping Through the Door 5

"But the others looked in the face of Aslan and loved him. . . .
And all these came in at the Door, in on Aslan's right."
The Last Battle
"At present, we are on the outside of the world,
the wrong side of the door. . . .
We cannot mingle with the splendours we see. . . .
Some day, God willing, we shall get *in*."
The Weight of Glory 13

Longing

This book has described why Lewis chose the fairy tale as the ideal form for what he had to say in his Narnia tales; this chapter describes the effects of this form. Fantasy satisfies our desires, especially the desire to escape death and experience a "happy ending."

For Lewis, marvelous literature evoked and satisfied his intense longing. In *The Weight of Glory*, Lewis says we all have a desire for a "far off country" like an inconsolable secret—"a desire for something that has never actually appeared in our experience" (4). We mistakenly identify what we long for as beauty or a memory; but these are only the "scent of a flower we have not found, the echo of a tune we have not heard, news from a country we have never yet visited" (5). What more poignant illustration of this could there be than the magical tree from Narnia that grows in Digory's back yard but bends whenever a breeze blows in Narnia because of the Narnian sap running within it.

As described in *Surprised By Joy*, Lewis all his life experienced this longing for a beauty that lies "on the other side" of existence, as do many of his characters. In Narnia, the things we long for are associated with the North, Aslan, the distant mountains of Aslan's country, and the islands of the Utter East.

Long before he even enters Narnia, Digory longs for a world with a fruit that could cure his sick mother. Similarly, Shasta says he has been "longing to go to the north all my life." "Of course you have," Bree responds. "That's because of the blood that's in you. . . . You're true northern stock." Not only is he returned to his home but also restored to his proper name.

Raised a Telmarine, and hearing only fleeting stories about Talking Narnians, Caspian searches for such people all his life. Caspian says to the children, "Sometimes I did wonder if there really was such a person as Aslan: but then I sometimes wondered if there were really people like you. Yet there you are."

His old nurse says that she, too, has always waited for Aslan. As Aslan leads his band of rejoicing, newly-freed followers through the town, a school teacher feels a "stab of joy" and follows him. Jill feels a similar sensation as she steps into Narnia through a hole in the wall; though frightened, she realizes she has "always been longing for something like this."

In *The Last Battle*, Jewel the Unicorn, upon reaching the new Narnia of Aslan's country, stamps on the ground and cries, "I have come home at last! This is my real country! I belong here. This is the land I have been looking for all my life, though I never knew it till now. The reason why we loved the old Narnia is that it sometimes looked a little like this." For Reepicheep, questing valiantly for the End of the World, the spell of Aslan's country "has been on me all my life."

Longing, says Lewis, is "*askesis*," or a spiritual exercise. He explains that because we want to be united with and receive beauty, "we have peopled air and earth and water with gods and goddesses and nymphs and elves—that although we cannot, yet these projections can, enjoy in themselves that beauty, grace, and power of which Nature is the image" (*Weight* 13). Such creatures present to us an old reality we have forgotten, help us see nature and man in a visionary way, and illustrate the idea of hierarchy and cosmic order.

A key theme in his books is therefore showing that there is more to reality than what we see. Lewis observes that "giants, dragons, paradises, gods, and the like are themselves the expression of certain basic elements in man's spiritual experience. In that sense they are more like words—the words of a language which speaks the else unspeakable" (*Preface* 57). The creatures in Narnia come straight out of the pages of classical mythology: giants, centaurs, unicorns, dwarfs, fauns, naiads, and dryads. The trees can hear and even assume human form: "strangely branchy and leafy" birch-girls, beech-girls, larch-girls; shaggy, wizened and hearty oak men with frizzled beards; lean and melancholy elms; and shockheaded hollies. Even common animals like foxes, badgers, mice, moles and squirrels are larger than in our world. As in the legends of the North American Indians, even the stars, like Coriakin and Ramandu, are glistening real people, with white hot spears and whose long hair shines like burning silver.

Are fairy stories merely escapism or wish fulfillment then? No, says Lewis. Instead, their true significance lies in their ability to arouse in one's mind a longing for something:

> A longing for he knows not what. It stirs and troubles him (to his life-long enrichment) with the dim sense of something beyond his reach and, far from dulling or emptying the actual world, gives it a new dimension of depth. He does not despise real woods because he has read of enchanted woods: the reading makes all real woods a little enchanted. This is a special kind of longing. (*On Stories* 38)

Furthermore, says Lewis, fairy stories not only present to us a whole spectrum of experiences in concrete form but, in giving us experiences we never had before, add to our lives. So although the tales may not be exactly like real life, they may show us what reality may be like "at some more central region."

Writer as Creator

Because Lewis believed everything originates with God, imaginative inventions must reflect God's Truth. There can therefore be no genuine creativeness because one can only reflect the universe's order and beauty: "I think that all things in their way, reflect heavenly truth, the imagination not least. 'Reflect' is the important word. This lower life of the imagination is not a beginning of nor a step towards, the higher life of the spirit, merely an image" (*Surprised* 167). The author should try to embody in art "some reflection of eternal beauty and Wisdom" (*Christian Reflections* 6-7). Lewis says poets, musicians, and inventors never "make," only build from, rearrange, and recombine elements and materials that already exist from the Creator (*Malcolm* 73, 203).

Lewis and Tolkien disagreed about the relation of art to God's Truth. According to Lewis, while man can create, he cannot do so from nothing as God can. Stories can only rearrange or retell what already exists. Tolkien, however, took a more liberal view of the idea of man being made in God's image. He called the artist a "sub-creator," i.e., a creator of images not found in our world. Lewis looks back to the One Story God has already created; Tolkien looks forward to the Truth as a story still in the making.

According to Tolkien, man is a "subcreator" when he creates a fantasy world:

> Although now long estranged,
> Man is not wholly lost nor wholly changed.
> Dis-graced he may be, yet is not de-throned,
> and keeps the rags of lordship once he owned:
> Man, Sub-creator, the refracted Light
> through whom is splintered from a single White
> to many hues, and endlessly combined
> in living shapes that move from mind to mind.

Though all the crannies of the world we filled
with Elves and Goblins, though we dared to build
Gods and their houses out of dark and light,
and sowed the seed of dragons—twas our right
(used or misused). That right has not decayed:
we make still by the law in which we're made ("On Fairy Stories"
74).

Man thus creates because he is made in the image of the Creator and because there is a part of him that is unsatisfied by the rational, natural world. Using materials from the world around him and drawing on spiritual reality, he expresses truths that cannot be expressed or explained in any other way. But to create convincing "other worlds," Lewis believed that he must draw on the only real "other world" he knows, that of the spirit.

Dream and Reality

The theme of what is real runs throughout the Narnia books. When Peter argues that if things are real, then they must be there all the time, Professor Kirke replies, "Are they?" Rather, there is the possibility of other worlds just around the corner.

When the children first hear the name "Aslan" for the first time, Lewis says that sometimes in a dream someone says something that seems to have "a lovely meaning, too lovely to put into words, which makes the dream so beautiful that you remember it all your life and are always wishing you could get into that dream again."

Digory experiences the same strange "echo" during his first time in the Wood Between the Worlds: "If anyone had asked him: 'Where did you come from?' he would probably have said, 'I've always been here.' That was what it felt like —as if one had always been in that place." His and Polly's life before this seems like a dream, a "picture" in their heads. The former life of Strawberry the horse also seems muddled like a dream, and Aslan's song reminds them all of "something." After the four Pevensies are Kings and Queens in Narnia for many years, the "real" world seems like a dream to them, too. As the Telmarine in *Prince Caspian* feels the touch of Aslan's breath, a new look comes into his eyes, "as if he were trying to remember something."

Only Aslan is able to "wake up" the visitors from earth to the reality he alone can bring. The children only need to look into his face to feel as though they have never been alive or awake before. In *The Horse and His Boy,* Shasta thinks his encounter with Aslan is a dream, but he sees the paw print that fills with water. After Aslan visits with the children, they feel as if awakened from sleep: "But there was a brightness in the air and on the grass, and a joy in their hearts, which assured them that he had been no dream."

In contrast, evil makes us forget. The White Witch cannot even remember being in the Wood Between the Worlds—that "quiet place"—no matter how often or how long she was there. Likewise, the gnome, Golg, says that the Green Witch called them to her world by magic and made them forget about their own world: "We didn't know who we were or where we belonged. We couldn't do anything, except what she put into our heads." Once freed, Golg says that he has newly remembered himself.

The Green Witch, who can make things look like what they are not, also convinces the children and Puddleglum that Narnia is just a dream. Puddleglum must denounce her evil, drowsy enchantment, which lures them into forgetting the real world. He reasons that if they have dreamed up everything, including Aslan, then "the made-up things seem a good deal more important than the real ones." While enchanted, Rilian cannot even remember his real self. On the other hand, once they leave her world, Underland seems like a dream.

Platonism

The children go further up (to Aslan's country in the mountains) and further in, then on to a garden containing a Narnia that is even better. From the mountains, they at last see a Narnia that is "as different as a real thing is from a shadow or as waking life is from a dream. . . . It's all in Plato," Professor Kirke explains. The children thus find the real Narnia and real England of which the others were only a shadow or copy. In fact, Aslan calls England the "Shadow-Lands."

Lewis's view of reality, involving man's separation from his heavenly potential, can be described as Platonic. Briefly, Plato believed that the real, stable, permanent part of the universe exists in a supernatural, super-sensible "heaven" as Ideas for Forms. The physical world is only the realm of appearances rather than solid reality—illusory, transitory. In this way, it is only a shadow or copy of the "real" world.

Lewis totally reverses the shadowy Platonic conception of heaven. We often tend to associate God and Heaven with the "sky" and the "spiritual," forgetting that our language is only symbolic and incapable of describing or understanding them. Consequently, says Lewis, God has become to many "like a gas diffused in space" or a "mist streaming upward"—vaporous, vague, indefinable, shadowy. We also have a "vague dream of Platonic paradises and gardens of the Hesperides" that represent the "heaven" we long for.

Although we associate spirit with ghosts and shadows, instead, spirit should be presented as "*heavier* than matter" because the Almighty is "concrete Fact" (*Miracles* 95). One purpose of creating other worlds is to show the reality of the spiritual world by characters attempting to come to terms with it. Lewis places his Platonic reality not in a far removed, abstract heaven, but rather at the very heart, the center of all that exists.

Near the End of the World, "Every leaf stood out so sharp that you'd think you could cut your finger on it." Similarly, in *The Last Battle*, the Platonic realm is portrayed as a solid, concrete reality. Lewis explains the difference as being like a reflection of a landscape in a mirror, where the reflection is just as real but "somehow different—deeper, more wonderful, more like places in a story." This "new Narnia" looks "deeper"—as if every flower and blade of grass "meant more." Lewis writes, "If you are tired of the real landscape, look at it in a mirror. By putting bread, gold, horse, apple, or the very roads into a myth, we do not retreat from reality: we rediscover it" (*On Stories* 90).

In *The Great Divorce,* Lewis likewise notes that in comparison to the ghostly earthlings stumbling on heaven's soil, things in heaven are much "solider," even harder in comparison—you can cut your finger on the grass. Life is weak and flimsy compared to the solid reality it reflects. Similarly, in *Perelandra*, Ransom is told, "You see only an appearance, small one. You have never seen more than an appearance of anything." He sadly realizes "I have lived all my life among shadows and broken images."

Stable Door

Lewis uses the Stable Door not only in *The Last Battle* but also in several of his other writings as an image for the entrance to that Platonic reality that we have always longed for because we have vague Wordsworthian recollections of a past glory: "We long to be inside of some door which we have always seen from the outside. . . . to be at last summoned inside would be both glory and honour beyond all our merits and also the healing of that old ache." Some day, says Lewis, we shall again be permitted to "*get in* . . . pass in through Nature, beyond her, into that splendour which she fitfully reflects" (*Weight* 13). The world we dream of, or remember, or long for is not "made-up." In Aslan's country, beyond the Stable Door, "The dream is ended: this is the morning."

Lewis argues that when we try to convert Biblical images to abstract thought we fail because abstract thinking is just a "tissue of analogies." Metaphor, imagery, and analogy can convey God's reality and concreteness. The Bible itself is thus the source of many of the images used in fantasy because the supernatural world is portrayed by using concrete images and mingling the familiar with the unfamiliar. Examples of archetypal symbols are blood, dragons and beasts, light and darkness, sun, water, sea, river and fountain, gold, the city, birds, garden, tree, purifying fire, sinister forest, music, and cave. In addition, the inner world is made real and personal by giving it concrete form through characters and action.

In his image of heaven, Lewis brings together several rich Biblical images that tie all the books together. The children first enter Aslan's country through a Stable Door. The Stable seen from within and without are two different places. Through the door, the children see only darkness, the bonfire, and the disbelieving dwarfs squatting just inside it. Inside is Aslan's country. The Stable Door represents both death and the entrance to Aslan's country. "It seems then," says Tirian, smiling himself, "that the Stable seen from within and the Stable seen from without are two different places." "Yes," says Lord Digory. "Its inside is bigger than its outside."

It is interesting that Shift had first used this Stable for his false Aslan and later that Tash hides within it. Lewis may here be illustrating his belief that many Pagan and false religions in a sense "prefigure" Christianity, containing elements of truth, even pointing the way to the real God.

Jesus warns what events will signal his return and the end of the world:

> When you hear of wars beginning, this does not signal my return; these must come, but the end is not yet. The nations and kingdoms of the earth will rise against each other. . . you will be tortured and killed and hated all over the world because you are mine, and many of you shall fall back into sin and betray and hate each other. And many false prophets will appear and lead many astray (Matthew 24:4-11).

How similar this account is to the changes Narnia undergoes in its final days. Shift's mock-Aslan is an almost ridiculous anti-Christ figure. There are false rumors about Aslan; talking animals are sold into slavery and hard labor; there are wars and betrayals. The centaur says that the stars do not prophecy the coming of Aslan but rather the coming evil.

In Matthew 24:29-31, Jesus describes the end of the earth:

> Immediately after the persecution of those days the sun will be darkened, and the moon will not give light, and the stars will seem to fall from the heavens, and the powers overshadowing the earth will be convulsed. . . . And I shall send forth my angels with the

> "And all the creatures who looked at Aslan in that way swerved to their right, his left, and disappeared into his huge black shadow. . . . But the others looked in the face of Aslan and loved him. . . . And all these came in at the Door, in on Aslan's right."
>
> *The Last Battle*

sound of a mighty trumpet blast, and they shall gather my chosen ones from the farthest ends of the earth and heaven.

The end of Narnia is much like this. Father Time blows his horn, producing each change in the landscape, just as Aslan's song had created it. First comes a downpouring of stars, leaving the sky empty. Aslan's acceptance into his country of those animals truly faithful to him is like a final judgment scene: those who love him pass by him, to his right, into the Door. Those who hate and fear him cease to be Talking Animals, passing to his left and into his enormous and terrible Shadow. Likewise, Jesus said, "I am the Door: by Me if any man enter in He shall be saved" (John 10:9).

Dragons and Giant Lizards devour Narnia as in the "Ragnarok" or destruction of the earth in Norse mythology. A wall of water rises to cover the earth. The red and dying sun and moon burn to nothing, creating a steam that rises from the blood-red waters. Similarly, in Acts 2:19-20, Jesus prophesies, "I will show wonders in the heaven above and signs on the earth beneath, blood, and fire, and vapor of smoke; the sun shall be turned into darkness and the moon into blood."

At last, Peter closes and locks the door on a cold, dead world. Jill Pole remarks, "*Our* world is going to have an end some day. Perhaps this one won't. Wouldn't it be lovely if Narnia just went on and on. . .?" But "all worlds draw to an end; except Aslan's country."

Aslan's Country

The disappointed children follow Aslan "further up and further in" through the Stable. The land just inside the door reminds them of something they can't quite place: a deep blue sky, soft summer breeze, and thick trees with wonderful, indescribable fruit that makes all the fruit of our world seem dull by comparison. It seems to be a country where everything is allowed.

Then they realize where they have seen all this before. Aslan's world is just like the Narnia they had known only "more like the real thing." They can see not only the layout of Narnia—the desert, Tashbaan, Cair Paravel, island after island to the End of the World—but even England looking like a cloud cut off from them by a gap. This, too, is the "England within England, the real England just as this is the real Narnia." All real countries, in fact, are like spurs jutting out from the great mountains of Aslan that ring the entire world.

In *Miracles*, Lewis compares nature to a witch who must eventually die. But it will be redeemed and cured. "We shall still be able to recognize our old enemy, friend, playfellow and foster-mother, so perfected as to be not less, but more, herself" (68).

What will our resurrected bodies be like? Lewis suggests that we will look the same, only better, just as the lands the children see in Aslan's country are the reality of which Narnia and England were incomplete reflections. The first effect on the children is that they

> "Jill. . . was going up the Waterfall herself. . . . You went on, up and up, with all kinds of reflected lights flashing at you from the water and all manner of coloured stones flashing through it, till it seemed as if you were climbing up light itself."
>
> *The Last Battle*

simply *feel* different—not sleepy, hungry, or thirsty. Like their vigor after the romp with Aslan following his resurrection, they feel life to its fullest.

One thing Lewis does, perhaps better than any other writer, is to depict a vision of what heaven is like. There are hints of Aslan's country in both *The Voyage of the "Dawn Treader"* and *The Silver Chair*. Quite unforgettable is the description of the End of the World in *The Voyage of the "Dawn Treader,"* always associated with the Utter East.

A wall stands up between them and the sky. Through it they see the sun turning into a rainbow of colors. This wall is really a 30-foot wave fixed in one place just like the edge of a waterfall.

In the distance, the mountains of a green, forested country "outside the world" come into view; these are always associated with Aslan's country in the Chronicles. After their unforgettable experience at the End of the World, Edmund and Lucy cannot describe the smell and the musical sound carried on the sweet breeze from Aslan's country: " 'It would break your heart.' 'Why,' said I, 'was it so sad?' 'Sad!! No,' said Lucy."

Two things they notice are also associated with Aslan himself: light and smell. The light becomes a whiteness

A Guide Through Narnia

radiating all around them, for the sun grows larger. Still, they get used to it, seeing "more light than they had ever seen before." Also, a "fresh, wild, lonely smell that seemed to get into your brain" pervades the air and gives energy. The clear water reveals a submarine world and is sweet like the air—like "drinkable light"—and carpeted with lilies. They feel cool, fresh, clean, and beautiful and wear only comfortable clothes. There is a stillness . . . and joy. To send the children back home, Aslan rips the blue wall like a curtain being torn and opens a door into the sky.

In *The Silver Chair*, Jill and Eustace are permitted to get just a taste of this country. They find a stream and crystal air that clears their minds, as well. When they return there briefly at the end of the book, Jill notices that this is a place where you can't want the wrong things, and people are no particular age. Aslan promises they some day may be called to this place—their real "home"—to stay forever.

In *The Last Battle*, the children are indeed called home. Able to run faster without getting hot or tired, the group moves even "further up and further in" through Aslan's country by scaling a waterfall. (This is most likely the "real" waterfall of which the Great Waterfall and Caldron Pool in the Lantern Waste had been only a reflection). Racing to an area just like the Western Wilds then up a hill, they enter a garden (again, just like the Platonic Ideal). They notice again the delicious smell and the springy turf dotted with white flowers. Even more wonderful, everyone they have ever heard of or loved and thought dead is there—except Susan, of course.

As Lucy climbs up the green slopes and mountains of forests, through the sweet orchards and past flashing waterfalls, she begins to see more and more clearly. Lucy finds that whatever she looks at, no matter how far away, becomes "quite clear and close as if she were looking through a telescope." Peering over the wall of the garden, she distinctly sees "Narnia" spread out below.

"I see," Lucy says thoughtfully. "I see now. This garden is like the stable. It is far bigger inside than it was outside." "Of course, Daughter of Eve," explains Mr. Tumnus. "The further up and further in you go, the bigger everything gets. The inside is larger than the outside." Lucy sees then, that the garden a whole world: "I see," she says. "This is still Narnia, and more real and more beautiful than the Narnia down below, just as it was more real and more beautiful than the Narnia outside the Stable door. I see. . . world within world, Narnia within Narnia. . . ." "Yes," says Mr. Tumnus, "like an onion: except that as you continue to go in and in, each circle is larger than the last." Lewis compares the Stable to the stable where Christ was born. Lucy comments: "In our world, too, a Stable once had something inside it that was bigger than our whole world."

The paradox implicit in the idea of a sphere with a center bigger than its circumference illustrates how difficult it is for us to believe that this vast universe came out of something smaller and emptier than itself:

> We are much nearer to the truth in the vision seen by Julian of Norwich, when Christ appeared to her holding in His hand a little thing like a hazel nut and saying, "This is all that is created." And it seemed to her so small and weak that she wondered how it could hold together at all. (*God in the Dock* 37)

In *Letters to Malcolm*, Lewis uses a similar image to describe what will happen to the resurrected soul. Although we now think of the soul as "inside the body," the glorified resurrection body—"the sensuous life raised from its death—will be inside the soul. As God is not in space but space is in God" (122).

The hill and garden that appears just inside the Stable Door and later "further up and further in" Aslan's country is the perfect garden, the image of which Digory had entered to obtain the apple. Digory had seen a bird sitting in the tree, larger than an eagle, with saffron breast, head crested with scarlet, and a purple tail; here we learn that it is a Phoenix. The Phoenix is a mythological bird larger than an eagle with brilliant gold and reddish purple feathers. At the end of its 500 year life cycle, it is said to burn itself on a funeral pyre. Another Phoenix then rises from the ashes with renewed youth and beauty. This traditional symbol of rebirth and immortality is fitting for the conclusion—or shall we say, the real beginning—of the children's adventures.

> "And the sea in the mirror, or the valley in the mirror, were in one sense just the same as the real ones: yet at the same time they were somehow different—deeper, more wonderful, more like places in a story: in a story you have never heard but very much want to know."
> *The Last Battle*

The Happy Ending

The only way to enter Aslan's country is by dying (*Letters to Children* 45). The Chronicles have one of the most unusual endings in children's books: the children and their parents die in a railway accident in England. Aslan tells the children: "all of you are—as you used to call it in the Shadow-lands—dead." The children's end on earth is the beginning of an even greater and never ending Story. The children "all lived happily ever after. But for them it was only the beginning of the real story." The Chronicles thus have the fairy tale ending Tolkien describes in his essay "On Fairy Stories." Tolkien says that fairy tales satisfy our "oldest and deepest desire": Escape from Death.

In *The Lion*, we have a foreshadowing of the victory of death when the Stone Table cracks and Death starts "working backwards." In *The Magician's Nephew*, Digory feeds his dying mother the Apple of Life that heals her. In *The Silver Chair*, we join the children in a wonderful glimpse of the afterlife in Aslan's country, and the means by which one can truly experience it. During Caspian's funeral in Narnia, the children are taken to Aslan's Mountain to walk by the stream. Then, in a striking image of the saving power of Christ's blood and the thorns that pierced his brow, Eustace is told to drive a thorn into Aslan's paw. The blood splashes onto the dead Caspian.

The miraculous change begins as we see death truly working backward, fulfilling the Deeper Magic. His white beard, sunken cheeks, and wrinkles vanish; his eyes open. Suddenly, he leaps up and stands before them. Knowing he has died, they think he is a ghost, just as Lucy and Susan had thought Aslan a ghost when he appeared before him after his sacrifice. But "one can't be a ghost in one's own country." Caspian now has the freedom of no longer wanting or doing the wrong things, and of never being afraid. This is his real home now. The children have been promised that they too will come here to stay one day.

Another more important element in fairy tales is what Tolkien calls the Consolation of the Happy Ending or Eucatastrophe: "a sudden glimpse of the underlying reality or truth" ("On Fairy" 70-1).

Myth gives a gleam of the Gospel in which the Eucatastrophe is true. Lewis calls Myth "at its best, a real though unfocussed gleam of divine truth falling on human imagination" (*Miracles* 139). Before his conversion, Lewis realized that pagan stories hinted at truth that later became history in the Incarnation. Yet he could not understand the purpose of Christ, the crucifixion, and resurrection. His friends Tolkien and Hugo Dyson replied that since he was affected by the sacrifice in pagan mythology, why not accept it in Christianity? When Lewis called myth lies, Tolkien objected. We invent terms for objects based on our perception of them. Through discussions with his friends, Lewis decided that the Christian story is a myth like other great myths. The difference is that the Bible is true: myth become fact. Art and imagination are a path to understanding and worshiping God. Because there is an objective, eternal Truth, God's "story" is already complete.

The Gospels themselves tell the greatest Story of all, the Eucatastrophe of the Resurrection, producing a tearful Christian joy by mingling Joy and Sorrow. This joy at the end of the story is a fundamental principle. In the Bible, writes Tolkien, is a story with all the characteristics of good fantasy—the marvelous, eucatastrophe, and consistency—and it is true:

> The Resurrection is the eucatastrophe of the story of the Incarnation. This story begins and ends in joy. It has pre-eminently the "inner consistency of reality." There is no tale ever told that man would rather find was true. ("On Fairy" 71-2)

In one of the most memorable passages in all of the Chronicles, Lucy, in reading the Magician's Magic Book, comes across a "spell for the refreshment of the spirit." Like the living pictures that Orual sees while telling Psyche's story at the end of *Till We Have Faces*, Lucy finds that she is living in the story as if it were real, and all the pictures were real, too. It is about a cup, a sword, a tree, and a green hill, and is the loveliest story she has ever read. But she can neither go back and read it again, nor really remember it. Ever since that time, though, Lucy defines a good story as one that reminds her of this forgotten story. Aslan, who is said to be "at the back of all the stories," promises her that he will tell that story to her for years and years.

The children can now begin the Great Story:

for them it was only the beginning of the real story.
All their life in this world and all their adventures in Narnia
had only been the cover and the title page:
now at last they were beginning Chapter One of the Great Story,
which no on on earth has read:
which goes on for ever;
in which every chapter is better than the one before.

Appendix

Dictionary of Names and Places in the Chronicles of Narnia

KEY:
( ) after name cites book in which name predominantly appears
LWW-The Lion, the Witch and the Wardrobe
VDT-The Voyage of The Dawn Treader
SC-The Silver Chair
MN-The Magician's Nephew
PC-Prince Caspian
LB-The Last Battle
HHB-The Horse and His Boy

SOURCES:
(OED) Oxford English Dictionary
(BDPF) Brewer's Dictionary of Phrase and Fable
(EDEL) An Etymological Dictionary of the English Language

ADELA PENNYFATHER (SC) One of the children at Experiment House.

AHOSHTA TARKAAN (HHB) Grand Vizier of Calormen; 60 years old, with a hump on his back, a face like an ape, and of base birth. Aravis' stepmother has arranged that she marry him.

ALAMBIL (PC) Planet whose name means Lady of Peace; its conjunction with the star Tarva means good fortune for Narnia.

ALBATROSS (VDT) Seabird. In ancient times, sighting the bird, an incarnation of a drowned seaman, was a warning of a storm ahead. Killing the bird would doom the ship and crew. Aslan takes the form of an albatross to help Lucy.

ALBERTA SCRUBB (VDT) Eustace's mother. "Up-to-date and advanced," she and her husband are vegetarians, non-smokers, teetotallers, and wear special underclothes. They think Eustace becomes tiresome under the influence of the Pevensies.

ALIMASH (HHB) Aravis' cousin, Captain of the Chariots and Calormene nobleman.

ANDREW KETTERLEY (MN) Digory's uncle, a dabbler in magic, who gets Digory and Polly Plummer into Narnia by means of magic rings. He is tall and thin, has a sharp nose and mop of grey hair, and mismanages money.

ANNE FEATHERSTONE (VDT) Lucy's friend whom she hears talking to Marjorie Preston under a spell in the Magician's Book; Lucy desires to hear what they think about her.

ANRADIN TARKAAN (HHB) a Tarkaan, Bree's master, who treated him badly and tries to buy Shasta. "Anrad" means having a single aim or purpose (OED).

ANVARD (HHB) Castle of the King of Archenland.

ARAVIR (PC) Morning star of Narnia.

ARAVIS TARKEENA (HHB) Tarkheena, the only daughter of Kidrash Tarkaan and descended from the god Tash; runs away from home because her stepmother has arranged for her marriage to Ahoshta. Marries Cor and becomes Queen of Archenland.

ARCHENLAND (MN, HHB) Country just south of Narnia below the Southern Mountains.

ARDEEB TISROC (HHB) Tisroc descended from Tash—an ancestor of Aravis' father.

ARGOZ (VDT) (see SEVEN LORDS).

ARLIAN (PC) One of Caspian IX's lords, executed by usurper Miraz for treason.

ARSHEESH (HHB) Calormene fisherman who raises Shasta.

ASLAN Son of the Emperor-Over-Sea (or Emperor Beyond-the-Sea), King and Creator of Narnia, the Great Lion. "Arslan" is the word for lion in Turkish (according to Walter Hooper). Aslan has nine names.

ASLAN'S COUNTRY (PC, VDT, SC, LB) Aslan's home (heaven) to which all countries are connected.

ASLAN'S HOW (PC) Huge mound in the Great Woods with hollowed galleries and caves; the Stone where Aslan was sacrificed is in the central cave.

ASLAN'S TABLE (VDT, LB) Table of renewal located on Ramandu's Island where a banquet appears each night and must be eaten before morning.

AVRA (VDT) Lone Island #3; few people live there; the location of Lord Bern's estates.

AXARTHA TARKAAN (HHB) Grand Vizier of Calormen before Ahosta Tarkaan.

AZAROTH (HHB) Calormene goddess.

AZIM BALDA (HHB) Calormene city where many roads meet and where the House of Imperial Posts is located.

AZROOH (HHB) A Calormene; one of Rabadash's Tarkaan lords from the eastern provinces, killed by Lune.

BACCHUS (PC) The god of wine from Greek and Roman mythology. Known also by the names Bromios, Basareus, and Ram. Lewis portrays him as a youth in fawn-skin, with vine leaves in his curly hair. In myth, he was a youth with black eyes and flowing locks.

BAR (HHB) King Lune's chancellor, a traitor, who kidnapped Cor when he heard he would save Archenland; later killed in battle.

BASSAREUS (PC) Wild boy (see BACCHUS).

BEAVERS (LWW, LB) Mr. and Mrs. Beaver help the children escape from the White Witch. Mr. Beaver tells the children about Aslan and the White Witch. He is hard-working and proud of his dam. Mrs. Beaver is very practical; she packs food for them to eat and even wants to take along her sewing machine.

BEAVERSDAM (LWW, PC, VDT, HHB) Town with a waterfall ruled by Telmarine Lords, the Brothers of Beaversdam.

BELISAR (PC) One of Caspian IX's lords who, under usurper Miraz, was shot intentionally with arrows on a hunting party. Belisarius was the greatest of the Emperor Justinian's generals, accused of conspiring, imprisoned, then restored to favor 6 months later, but his eyes were eventually put out (BDFM).

BERN (VDT) (see SEVEN LORDS) "Berne, Beorn" means warrior or hero (OED).

BERNSTEAD (VDT) Bern's estate on Avra.

BERUNA (LWW, SC) Town in Narnia inhabited primarily by Telmarines. Famous for its bridge, fords, and two battles. "Berun" means to run or flow over the surface (OED). Aslan's forces camp here the night of Aslan's sacrifice. The bridge is destroyed under Aslan's command to free the river god.

BETTY (LWW) Along with Ivy and Margaret, one of Digory Kirke's servants.

BIG BANNISTER (SC) One of the children at Experiment House.

BISM (SC) Enchanted subterranean land beneath the Witch's ShallowLands. Associated with gnomes and salamanders, heat and fire, an intoxicating smell, and live gems. Because the gnomes plunge headlong into it, Lewis may be associating it with the heart of reality. "Bism" probably comes from "Bisme," meaning abyss or deep pit (OED). Based on medieval belief that gnomes live in subterranean fire.

BLACK WOODS (PC) Great Woods located near the sea and the site of Cair Paravel. The Telmarine rumor is that the woods are full of ghosts because the Telmarines fear the sea and let the woods grow as protection from it.

BOGGLES (LWW) Evil spirits.

BRAMANDIN (MN) Dead world like Charn.

BREE (HHB) Narnian, dappled war-horse who is stolen and becomes Tarkaan Anradin's horse in Calormen. Runs away with Shasta. He is a skeptic who needs proof that Aslan is a real lion. "Bree" is short for Breehy-hinny-brinny-hoohy-hah, which sounds like the bray of a horse, but can also means disagreement (OED).

BRENN, ISLE OF (VDT) One of the Seven Isles, where Redhaven is located.

BRICKLETHUMB (HHB) A Red Dwarf, one of Duffle's two brothers, who feeds Shasta when he first enters Narnia. "Brickle" means fragile, delicate (OED).

BROMIOUS (PC) (see BACCHUS)

BUFFIN (LWW) Giant clan.

BULGY BEARS (PC) Three of the Old Narnians; sleepy bears who offer Caspian honey. One is Marshal of the Lists during Peter's fight with Miraz. "Bulgy" means swollen or clumsy (OED).

BURNT ISLAND (VDT) Island where children find a few animals and ruins of stone huts blackened by fires; they also find tiny boat there for Reepicheep.

CABBY (MN) Cab-driver in London who enters Narnia with the children and Witch by mistake, later becomes King Frank (first King of Narnia); illustrates how a lowly person can become King.

CAIR PARAVEL (LWW, PC, SC, LB) Castle and capital of Narnia. A "Court Paravail" is an inferior or lower court; a "Paravail" is one in a position below another but who holds another beneath like a tenant. Lewis is thus implying that while the Kings and Queens rule over Narnia, they, in turn, are in submission to Aslan and the Emperor-Over-Sea.

CALAVAR (HHB) Province ruled by Kidrash Tarkaan, Aravis' father.

CALDRON POOL (LB) Big pool under the cliffs at the West end of Narnia; given that name because the water dances and bubbles in a churning motion.

CALORMEN (HHB) Country far south of Narnia and four times its size.

CALORMENE (HHB, LB) Native of Calormen; Calormenes are known for their dark faces and long beards. Wear flowing robes, orange turbans, are wise, courteous, cruel. Worship the god Tash and have a rigid hierarchy. "Calor" means heat or warmth (OED)—appropriate because they come from a southern climate; may also refer to "color" because of their dark skin or "heat" (Latin).

CAMILLO (PC) Talking hare who leads a group to the Great Council.

CARTER (SC) Student at Experiment House who tortures rabbits.

CASPIAN (VDT, SC, PC)

Caspian I of Telmar conquered Narnia and silenced the Beasts. He is the first Telmarine King of Narnia.

Caspian VIII is father of Caspian IX and Miraz.

Caspian IX is murdered by his brother Miraz.

Caspian X, "the Seafarer," defeats Miraz, then searches for his father's seven lost lords in VDT. He marries Ramandu's daughter, dies at the end of SC, but is seen resurrected in Aslan's country. Leads War of Deliverance.

The name Caspian was first used by Lewis in his poem version of *Till We Have Faces* (Green and Hooper).

CENTAUR (LWW, PC, SC, HHB) Creature in Greek and Roman mythology with the body of a horse and the head and chest of a man. Glenstorm, Cloudbirth, and Roonwit are centaurs.

CHARN (MN) Dead world ruled by Jadis the Witch; once the city of the King of Kings. Is a form of "churn," which means to agitate (OED).

CHERVY THE STAG (HHB) Meets Corin with the news of Calormen attack on Anvard.

CHIEF VOICE (VDT) Chief Duffer and Chief Monopod.

CHIPPINGFORD (LB) Town, site of marketplace in Narnia during the latter days.

CHLAMASH (HHB) A Calormene; one of Rabadash's Tarkaan lords who surrenders.

CHOLMONDELY MAJOR (SC) One of children at Experiment House.

CITY RUINOUS (SC) Ruins of a city near Harfang, beneath which is the Green Witch's kingdom. The Witch tells them that a king once ruled there who had inscribed on the stones: "Though under Earth and throneless now I be,/Yet, while I lived, all Earth was under me."

CLIPSIE (VDT) Chief of the Dufflepud's little daughter who spoke the spell to make the Dufflepuds invisible. "Clipsi" means dark (OED). Possibly related to "eclipse."

CLODSLEY SHOVEL (PC) Leader of the moles. Charlotte Yonge's autobiography describes her ancestor's embalming of Sir Cloudesley Shovel, a famous admiral.

CLOUDBIRTH (SC) Centaur and famous healer; he heals Puddleglum's burnt foot.

COALBLACK (SC) Prince Rilian's horse.

COL (MN) First King of Archenland and son of Frank.

COLE (HHB) Along with his brother COLIN, fights for King Lune against the Calormenes (also see DAR).

COLIN (see COLE)

COR (HHB) (SHASTA) Corin's twin brother and son of King Lune, who escapes from Calormen with Bree, Hwin, and Aravis and becomes King of Archenland. "Cor" means heart (Latin).

CORIAKIN (VDT) Magician and retired star who governs the Dufflepuds as a punishment.

CORIN (HHB) Cor's twin brother and son of King Lune, called Thunder-fist because he was a great boxer.

CORNELIUS (PC, VDT) Half-dwarf; Caspian's tutor who teaches him the true history of Narnia. Short and fat, with a long beard and wrinkled face.

CORRADIN OF CASTLE TORMUNT (HHB) One of Rabadash's Tarkaan lords from the eastern provinces, killed by Edmund.

DAR (HHB) Brother of Darrin. Both of these lords of Archenland fight against the Calormenes for King Lune. Obscure variation of "dare" (OED). Several sets of brothers fight for Lune who, in turn, has twin sons; e. g. Col/Colin, Dar/Darrin, Cor/Corin.

DARRIN (HHB) (see DAR)

DANCING LAWN (PC, SC) Location of Great Council of Caspian and his Narnian friends, as well as other councils and feasts.

DARK ISLAND (VDT) Island, appearing as dark spot in the ocean, where dreams come true.

DAWN TREADER (VDT) Galley-type ship children use to travel to the End of the World (thus appropriateness of name). Shaped like a dragon, with green sides and a purple sail. Lewis loved drawing detailed pictures of ships like this as a child.

DEATHWATER (VDT) Reepicheep's name for the island where the children discover a pool that turns all to gold.

DEEP MAGIC (LWW) Law of the Emperor-Over-Sea that says that unless the Witch is given blood for every treachery committed, all Narnia will be overturned and perish in fire and water. May represent Old Testament Law.

DEEPER MAGIC (LWW, VDT, LB) Deeper than the Deep Magic, this Law of the Emperor says that if a willing victim is killed in a traitor's stead, the Stone Table will crack and Death will start working backwards. May represent New Testament Grace.

DEPLORABLE WORD (MN) Secret word known only to the great kings; if spoken, it will destroy all living things except the one who speaks it. Jadis pays the price to learn it and speaks the word during a battle with her sister, thus putting herself and all of Charn into a frozen enchantment.

DESTRIER (PC) Caspian's horse; means "war-horse" or "charger" (OED).

DIGGLE (LB) One of the eleven dwarfs who don't believe in "anything but themselves" during *The Last Battle*. He is the one Tirian picks up in the Stable.

DIGORY KIRKE (LWW, MN, LB) As a boy, he visits his Uncle Andrew and is sent by magic into Narnia, where he is responsible for helping bring evil into it. Takes back an apple seed from which a tree grows and the magic wardrobe is eventually made. As an old professor, he has a famous mansion visited by sightseers. The four Pevensies visit him at his home and enter Narnia through his wardrobe. Later, he becomes poor and has to sell his home and tutor students. Lewis probably named him after his old tutor "Kirke" or William Kirkpatrick. But he is also probably modeled after Lewis himself. Kirke is described as the sort of person who wants to know everything.

D.L.F. (PC) Dear Little Friend, the nickname Edmund gives to Trumpkin the dwarf.

DOORN (VDT) Lone Island #2, where most of the people live.

DRAGON ISLAND (VDT) Island where Eustace becomes a dragon.

DRINIAN (SC, VDT) Caspian's captain on the "Dawn Treader."

DRYAD (LWW, PC, VDT, SC, HHB, MN, LB) Wood nymph from Greek and Roman mythology..

DUFFER (VDT) (see MONOPODS) Means "an incapable or foolish, stupid, inept, unproductive person" (OED).

DUFFLE (HHB) A "practical" Red Dwarf who feeds and cares for Shasta when he first enters Narnia. "Duffle" is thick woolen cloth (OED).

DUFFLEPUD (VDT) (see MONOPOD)

DUMNUS (PC) A faun.

DWARFS (MC, PC, LWW) Small legendary creatures, usually involved in mining. Narnia has red-haired and black-haired dwarfs, and they can be either good or bad.

EARTHMEN (SC) Creatures living in the Marches of Underland—probably gnomes. They all look different: some have tails, beards, round faces, long pointed noses, soft trunk-like noses, blobby noses, or horns on their foreheads; all look sad. Their real home is Bism.

EASTERN SEA (LWW, PC) Great ocean bordering all the countries on the east.

EDITH JACKLE (SC) One of the children at Experiment House—a mean, spiteful tale-bearer. Name reminiscent of "jackal."

EDITH WINTERBLOTT (SC) One of the children at Experiment House.

EDMUND PEVENSIE (LWW, VDT, HHB, PC, LB) Second youngest Pevensie child; "traitor" in LWW who is "converted" by Aslan and for whom Aslan is sacrificed.

EFREET (LWW) Evil spirit. An "afreet" or "afrit" is a powerful evil jinnee, demon, or monstrous giant.

ELEANOR BLAKISTON (SC) Child at Experiment House.

EMETH TARKAAN (LB) Calormene permitted into Aslan's country because all his worship of Tash is counted as Aslan's. Here Lewis may be illustrating his belief in many possible roads to God since Emeth is sincere in seeking truth. Lewis himself defined the word as meaning "truth, intrinsic validity, rock bottom reality, something rooted in God's own Nature." In Jewish religion and in Hebrew, "Emeth" means true and valid.

EMPEROR-OVER-SEA (LWW, PC, VDT, HHB, LB) Aslan's father; God. Also called Emperor-Beyond-the-Sea.

ERIMON (PC) One of Caspian IX's lords executed by usurper Miraz on a false charge of treason.

ERLIAN (LB) King of Narnia (Rilian's father) who died from fight with giant.

ETTINS (LWW) Evil giants. "Ettin" means giant.

ETTINSMOOR (SC) City north of the Shribble River, a desolate moorland near where the giants live. Years earlier, Caspian X fought the giants and made them pay tribute. The Green Witch says they are foolish, fierce, savage. Variant form of the word "Eten," meaning giant (OED).

EUSTACE CLARENCE SCRUBB (VDT, SC, LB) Selfish and egotistical son of Alberta and Harold Scrubb, student at Experiment House who read "the wrong kind of books." Turns into a dragon and is undragoned by Aslan.

EXPERIMENT HOUSE (SC) Eustace's and Jill's school. "Co-educational," where girls and boys are allowed to do what they like. Lewis seems to be attacking the theory of "democratic education," which demands equal education for all but results in inferior education for the intelligent.

FARSIGHT (LB) Eagle who reports downfall of Narnia to Tirian.

FATHER CHRISTMAS (LWW) Santa Claus figure who at last comes to Narnia when Christmas comes and gives gifts to the children (which they use later in their adventures) and to the animals.

FATHER TIME (SC, LB) A giant who was once a King in Overland but has sunk into the Deep Realm where he dreams of the Upper World. He awakes at the end of the world and helps end Narnia by blowing his horn. Is given a "new name" (Eternity?) when he is awakened. Traditionally, an old, white-bearded man carrying a scythe and hour-glass.

FAUN (PC) Woodland spirit from Greek and Roman mythology with the legs, ears and tail of a deer and the face and body of a man.

FELIMATH (VDT) The first Lone Island, where sheep are kept. Lonely place with lots of grass and clover.

FELINDA (MN) Dead world like Charn.

FENRIS ULF (LWW) (Called Maugrim in some editions). A wolf who is Captain of Jadis' Secret Police. This character is based on Fenrir (or Fenris), wolf of Loki in Scandinavian mythology. At Ragnarok (Twilight of the Gods), he swallowed Odin but was avenged by Vidar who stabbed him with a sword—just as Peter kills him with a sword.

FLEDGE (MN, LB) Cabby's horse Strawberry who enters Narnia by accident, along with the Witch and the Cabby, from London. Becomes the first flying horse in Narnia. "Fledge" means to acquire feathers large enough to fly or to be able to fly (OED).

FORDS OF BERUNA (see BERUNA)

FRANK (MN) (see CABBY)

GALE (LB) Ninth Narnian king in descent from King Frank. Sailed into the Eastern Seas and delivered the Lone Islanders from a dragon and thus was given the Lone Islands as part of Narnia.

GALMA (VDT) Caspian's first stop on his trip, an isle where the great tournament is held.

GARRETT TWINS (SC) Two of the children at Experiment House, described as "loathesome."

GENTLE GIANTS (SC) Giants living at Harfang who plan on eating the children. Witch calls them "mild, civil, prudent, courteous."

GHOUL (LWW, HHB) Evil spirit associated with the dead.

GIANTS (SC) Tall race that inhabits Harfang and Ettinsmoor. Rumblebuffin, Wimbleweather, and Stonefoot are good giants.

GINGER (LB) A tom-cat, one of Shift's counsellors who tells false stories about Aslan. Seems to illustrate "enlightenment" attitude by believing in no god at all. At the Kilns where Lewis lived were two cats, one a ginger named Tom.

GIRBIUS (PC) A faun.

GLASSWATER CREEK (PC) Creek that leads to the Hill of the Stone Table.

GLENSTORM (PC, LB) Centaur who lives in a mountain glen; a noble creature with glossy chestnut flanks and a golden red beard. Prophet and Stargazer.

GLIMFEATHER (SC, LB) Owl who is big as a dwarf. Works for aged Caspian X and looks after Jill and Eustace, carrying them to Parliament of Owls, then Northern Mountains. "Glim" means to shine, gleam (OED).

GLOZELLE (PC) One of Miraz's lords who plans Miraz's defeat in PC by tricking him into accepting Peter's challenge to duel. To "gloze" means to expound upon or interpret (OED), appropriate since Glozelle talks Miraz into accepting. He is the one who actually stabs Miraz.

GNOMES (SC) Inhabitants of Underworld and Bism. Short, fat, whitish, pig-like faces, with long tails, a hard comb on the tops of their heads, pink eyes, large mouths and chins.

GOLDWATER (VDT) Caspian's first name for Deathwater Island because of the pool there that turns things and people to gold.

GOLG (SC) Gnome from Bism who is captured by Puddleglum.

GRAND VIZIER (HHB) Calormene leader. In Persia and Turkey, this title usually signifies a high state official like the governor of a province (OED).

GREAT DESERT (HHB) Desert between Archenland (north) and Calormen (south).

GREAT RIVER (PC, LB) River leading to Aslan's How, which children search for in PC. Extends all the way from Lantern Waste in the west, across Narnia, to the Eastern Ocean.

GREAT WATERFALL (LB) Source of the Great River that pours into the Caldron Pool and is located on the western edge of Narnia.

GREAT WOODS (PC) Forest located in eastern Narnia called the Black Woods by the Telmarines.

GRIFFLE (LB) Chief of the dwarfs in LB who decide to fight for and believe only in themselves.

GUMPAS (VDT) Bilious, incompetent governor of the Lone Islands, who is dethroned by Caspian and replaced by Lord Bern. Parody of the politician who insists upon following schedules and appointments and who sticks to his statistics and graphs. A "gump" is a dolt, numbskull, foolish person (OED).

GWENDOLEN (PC) School girl in New Narnia who joins with Aslan's band of party-goers.

HAG (LWW, PC) Witches who bind Aslan on the Stone Table. A hag is Nikabrik's accomplice, with a nose and chin that stick out like nutcrackers, and dirty grey hair. Based on the evil spirit or demon, usually female and usually associated with the Furies and Harpies.

HARDBITERS (PC) Badgers who attend the Great Council.

HARFANG (SC) Stronghold of the Gentle Giants, where Jill, Eustace, and Puddleglum are fed, bathed—and almost eaten.

HAROLD SCRUBB (VDT) Eustace Scrubb's father (see ALBERTA).

HARPHA TARKAAN (LB) Father of Emeth, who is one of his seven sons; a Tarkaan.

HELEN (MN, LB) (Nellie) Wife of Frank the Cabby, first Queen of Narnia. A plain housewife who is yanked into Narnia with soapsuds still on her arms.

HERMIT OF SOUTHERN MARCH (HHB) Keeps the horses and the wounded Aravis while Shasta goes on his mission to warn King Lune. He is 109 years old, tall, with beard to his knees and a robe; has a magic pool (almost like a crystal ball).

HOGGLESTOCK (PC) Hedgehog at the Great Council. "Hoggle" is a laborer of the lower class (OED).

HWIN (HHB) Narnian talking horse taken as a slave in Calormen; escapes with Aravis.

HYALINE (SPLENDOUR) (HHB) Ship of King Edmund and Queen Lucy. "Hyaline" means transparent like glass (OED).

ILGAMUTH (HHB) A Calormene; one of Rabadash's Tarkaan lords; killed by Darrin.

ILKEEN (HHB) Location of the beautiful palace of Ahoshta Tarkeen.

ILSOMBREH TISROC (HHB) Aravis's great-great-grandfather.

ISLAND OF THE VOICES (VDT) Island where Dufflepuds live.

IVY (LWW) Along with Betty and Margaret, one of Digory Kirke's servants.

JACKDAW (MN) Black and gray bird of the crow family that talks during Aslan's creation when everyone else is silent.

JADIS (LWW, MN) A White Witch who in LWW is Queen of Narnia. She spoke the Deplorable Word, which destroyed her rival sister, and she rules a dead Charn in MN. Enters London by accident. Slays most of the inhabitants of Narnia, turns them to stone, and turns its season to perpetual winter. Tall and beautiful but proud, with snowwhite face and red mouth. Descended from Lilith and one of the Jinn on one side, a giant on the other. Lilith was Adam's first wife who became the devil's dam. Jinn were demons who were created before Adam and assumed many shapes. A "jade" is a contemptuous name for a woman; "jadish" means worn or wearied (OED); it means "witch" in Persian. Jardis was also the name for Psyche's twin brother in Lewis's poem version of *Till We Have Faces* (Green and Hooper).

JEWEL (LB) A Unicorn; Tirian's dearest friend. They loved each other and saved each other's lives in war. Has a blue horn.

JILL POLE (SC, LB) Child from Experiment House who goes with Eustace on two adventures to Narnia. Aslan tells her the four Signs.

KETTERLEY (see ANDREW)

KIDRASH TARKAAN (HHB) Aravis's father; son of Rishti Tarkaan, son of Kidrash Tarkaan, son of Ilsombreh Tisroc, son of Ardeeb Tisroc, descended from Tash.

KIRKE (LWW, MN, LB) (see DIGORY)

LADY LILN (HHB) The wife of King Olvin of Archenland.

LADY OF THE GREEN KIRTLE (SC) Tall witch dressed in a thin green garment and really the Green Witch. Has enchanted Rilian in her Shallow Lands. First appears to children as a lovely lady with her knight and tricks them into going to Harfang. Turns into a serpent (thus symbolic color green) and is perhaps a serpent or Satan symbol. A "kirtle" is a gown or coat (OED).

LAMP-POST (LWW) Lamp-post in Lantern Waste, the western boundary of Narnia. Jadis brings part of a lamp-post from England into Narnia and throws it at Aslan, but it falls and grows into a complete lamp-post that is always lit.

LANTERN WASTE (MN) Area west of Beaversdam where the children first enter Narnia, where the lamp-post grows, and where Jadis's kingdom is.

LAPSED BEAR OF STORMNESS (HHB) Talking bear who boxes with Corin.

LASARALEEN TARKHEENA (HHB) An old friend of Aravis, who helps her escape Tashbaan; a silly and vain Tarkheena, now married and great. Interested only in clothes, parties, and gossip. "Lasar" means leisure (OED).

LEFAY, MRS. (MN) In Lewis's original version of the story, Digory's godmother who has magic powers. In MN, she is Andrew's godmother and has fairy blood in her. Gives him a box of dust from Atlantis. Probably named after Morgan Le Fay, famous witch in the Arthurian legend with magical powers.

LETTY (LETITIA) KETTERLEY (MN) Uncle Andrew's sister, whom Jadis hurls across the room, but who seems unimpressed by the Witch.

LILITH (LWW) Wife of a Jinn and mother of the White Witch. In folklore, a female demon who was Adam's first wife.

LILYGLOVES (PC) Chief mole who helps plant the orchard at Cair Paravel.

LONE ISLANDS (VDT) Islands of FELIMATH, DOORN, and AVRA, which the "Dawn Treader" visits. King Gale of Narnia delivered their people from a dragon and was given these islands located east of Cair Paravel as part of Narnia. Although Lewis hints he may tell us this story in a future book, he never does.

LUCY PEVENSIE (LWW, VDT, HHB, PC, LB) Youngest of the four Pevensie children who is the first to visit through the wardrobe. Has task of saying a spell to make Dufflepuds visible. Seems to love, trust, and see Aslan more than anyone else. Undoubtedly named after Lucy Barfield, to whom LWW is dedicated (see letter at beginning of LWW).

LUNE (HHB) King of Archenland; Cor and Corin's father; fat and jolly.

MABEL KIRKE (MN) Digory's mother and sister of Andrew and Letitia Ketterley; sick, but cured by apple from Narnia.

MACREADY (LWW) Digory Kirke's housekeeper in his old country mansion. Probably based on Lewis's childhood housekeeper, Mrs. McCreedy.

MARCHES OF UNDERLAND, WARDEN OF (SC) Mullugutherum, chief of the Earthmen in the Underworld realm where the Green Witch rules.

MARGARET (LWW) Along with Betty and Ivy, one of Digory Kirke's servants.

MARJORIE PRESTON (VDT) Lucy's friend whom she overhears talking to Anne Featherstone under a spell from the Magician's book. Aslan says she is afraid of the older girl and really loves Lucy.

MARSHWIGGLE (SC) One of Lewis's most famous character creations. Long and frog-like creatures who do most of the watery and fishy work in Narnia; live in Wigwams in the marshes just north of Cair Paravel (see PUDDLEGLUM).

MASTER BOWMAN (VDT) Sailor on the "Dawn Treader" responsible for shooting at the Sea Serpent.

MAUGRIM (see FENRIS ULF)

MAVRAMORN (VDT) (see SEVEN LORDS)

MENTIUS (PC) A faun who dances for Caspian X.

MEZREEL (HHB) A resort for wealthy Calormenes with a lake, gardens, and Valley of the Thousand Perfumes.

MINOTAURS (LWW) In Greek mythology, a mythical monster with the head of a bull and the body of a man. Huge men with heads of bulls that fight for the White Witch.

MIRAZ (PC) Caspian IX's brother, a Telmarine who usurps the throne and casts out many of his lords. Caspian X overthrows him in battle. Murdered by his own lord, Glozelle.

MONOPOD (VDT)—also DUFFERS, DUFFLEPUDS. Creatures with one huge leg and foot like a mushroom, with curled toes. (Monopod means "one foot"). Once plain dwarfs, they were ruled by Magician Coriakin, who "uglified" them when they disobeyed him. Then, by a spell from his book, they made themselves invisible. They convinced Lucy to find a spell to make them visible again. They mimic everything their chief says and are very foolish and impractical. Lewis seems to have based them on the "Skiapod" written about in Medieval literature. A Medieval book, *The Bestiary*, which dates from the 13th century, outlines all the fanciful characteristics of various creatures. It describes a "skiapod," which possesses an enormous foot that it uses as a sunshade when lying on its back. Sir John Mandeville (*Travels*) describes the inhabitants of Ethiopia who have one foot: "And the foot is so large, that it shadoweth all the body against the sun; when they will lie and rest them."

MOONWOOD (LB) Hare who has such sensitive ears that he can sit by the Caldron Pool under the waterfall and hear what is whispered at Cair Paravel.

MOUNT PIRE (HHB) Mountain created when Fair Olvin fought the two-headed giant, Pire, and turned him to stone. Blue mountain with two peaks located northwest of the Tombs of the Ancient Kings. Shasta uses this as a landmark to find Archenland.

MUIL (VDT) Westernmost of the Seven Isles. Variation of the word "moil," which is a type of hornless cattle (OED). These were probably raised on the island.

MULLUGUTHERUM (SC) A gnome, the Warden of Marches of Underland (see MARCHES OF UNDERLAND).

NAIAD (LWW, PC, MN) Water nymph.

NAIN (PC) King of Archenland during Miraz's reign. "Nain" can mean highlander or "one's own" (OED).

NARNIA Aslan's country, created in MN and destroyed in LB, existing for almost 50 earth years, 2555 Narnian years. Land of Talking Beasts. According to Marjorie Wright, Narnia is the name of an Italian town mentioned by Livy. It was also mentioned at least seven times in Latin literature.

NARROWHAVEN (VDT) Town on Isle of Doorn where Gumpas rules.

NAUSUS (PC) A faun who dances for Caspian X.

NELLY (MN) Queen Helen of Narnia (see HELEN).

NIKABRIK (PC) Black Dwarf with black beard and hair. A sour Dwarf who goes against Caspian and tries to call on the Witch for help. Killed in a scuffle.

NIMIENUS (PC) A faun who dances for Caspian X.

NYMPH (LWW, PC, MN) Beautiful maiden who inhabits forests and bodies of water.

OBENTINUS (PC) A faun who dances for Caspian X.

OCTESIAN (VDT) (see SEVEN LORDS)

OLVIN (HHB) King of Archenland who defeats the giant Pire by turning him into stone, thus creating Mount Pire.

ORKNIES (LWW) Thin, mishievous monsters that serve the White Witch.

ORRUNS (SC) A faun.

OSCUNS (PC) A faun who dances for Caspian X.

PARAVEL (see CAIR PARAVEL)

PARLIAMENT OF OWLS (SC) A meeting of owls to which the children are carried on Glimfeather's back. Lewis is obviously having fun here, echoing a famous work by Chaucer called *The Parliament of Fowls*.

PASSARIDS (PC) House of Telmarine lords under Caspian IX. Under usurper Miraz, sent to fight giants and destroyed. "Passaree" is a nautical term (OED).

PATTERTWIG (PC) Magnificent red Squirrel, the size of a terrier, who can talk; one of the Old Narnian's whom Caspian meets and who offers him a nut from his store. Like most animals, his name is descriptive of the sound he makes. According to Walter Hooper, Pattertwig appears in the "LeFay Fragment," an early version of *The Magician's Nephew*.

PEEPICHEEK (PC) Second mouse under Reepicheep.

PERIDAN (HHB) One of Queen Susan's and King Edmund's lords and advisors in Tashbaan who leads charge in battle with Rabadash's army.

PETER PEVENSIE (LWW, PC, LB) Oldest Pevensie child, first High King of Narnia whom we meet after King Frank. Noted for his chivalry in battle. Too old to return to Narnia after PC. Probably named after the Biblical Peter, the rock on whom the church is built, and given keys to the kingdom in Matt. 16:19. Peter locks the door on dead Narnia.

PEVENSIE (LWW) Family name of Peter, Susan, Lucy, Edmund. In Rudyard Kipling's story *Puck of Pook's Hill*, a brother and sister live on an estate near a ruined castle by the sea called "Pevensey." In addition, Puck calls them "Son of Adam" and "Daughter of Eve."

PEVENSIE, MR. AND MRS. (LWW, VDT, LB) The parents of Peter, Susan, Edmund, and Lucy. Mr. Pevensie is a professor.

PHOENIX (MN, LB) Bird sitting in tree in center of Aslan's garden. Larger than an eagle, with gold and red-purple feathers. Symbol of rebirth and immortality because it is said to die and be resurrected from the ashes.

PITTENCREAM (VDT) Sailor of "Dawn Treader" left behind at Ramandu's Island. Went to live in Calormen and made up stories about the World's End.

PLATO (LWW, LB) Greek philosopher (5ᵗʰ c. B.C.) who believed that the real, stable, permanent part of the universe is the super-sensible world of Ideas or Forms. The physical world is a realm of appearances rather than reality and is thus illusory and transitory. It is a shadow or copy of the Real World.

POGGIN (LB) One of the first and only dwarfs in the LB who turns to Tirian's side against Shift and resists the temptation to believe him.

POLLY PLUMMER (MN) Digory's neighbor who enters Narnia with him in *The Magician's Nephew*.

POMELY (PC) Glozelle's horse.

POMONA (PC) Greatest of all wood people who puts a spell on the orchard at Cair Paravel. "Pomona" means goddess of fruits and fruit trees (OED).

PRIZZLE, MISS (PC) Teacher in a girl's school in Beruna.

PRUNAPRISMIA (PC) Miraz's red-haired wife and Caspian's aunt.

PUDDLEGLUM (SC) A marshwiggle, with long thin face, sharp nose and greeny-grey hair like reeds, long legs and arms, webbed feet and hands, wearing a high hat. Has a serious and pessimistic view of life, yet is "brave as a lion," level-headedly guiding the children in SC against the Green Witch. "Puddle" fits his marshy home; "glum" fits his mood. Lewis says the character was based on his gardener, Paxford.

PUG (VDT) One of Gumpas' slavers; a pirate. "Pug" can mean a number of things, including courtesan, upper servant, punk (OED).

PUGRAHAN (LB) Calormene salt mines.

PUZZLE (LB) Simple donkey who puts on false lion costume under Shift's orders but soon comes over to Tirian's side. His name fits not only the fact that he "puzzles" the Narnians by masquerading as Aslan, but he is also slow and confused about whom to believe.

QUEEN OF THE DEEP REALM/UNDERLAND (SC) Lady of the Green Kirtle, or the Green Witch, who has enchanted Rilian and rules the Shallow-Lands.

RABADASH (HHB) Son of Tisroc of Tashbaan who wants to marry Queen Susan. Attacks Archenland and is transformed by Aslan into a donkey.

RAM (PC) The Ram. Bacchus, the god of wine in Roman mythology. Also called Bromios and Bassareus.

RAM THE GREAT (HHB) Son of Cor and Aravis who becomes King of Archenland.

RAMANDU (VDT) A retired star, dressed all in silver, who resides near Aslan's Table. When he is rejuvenated by the berry provided by the birds, he will once again tread the Great Dance. Babylonian and Blackfoot Indian legends say that every star was once a human.

RAMANDU'S DAUGHTER (VDT, SC) Marries Caspian X. Falls asleep one day and is murdered by the Green Witch (a serpent).

RAMANDU'S ISLAND (VDT) Island of the Star, Island of the Three Sleepers. Island where Aslan's Table is located and Ramandu's home.

RAVEN OF RAVENSCAUR (PC) Leader of the Ravens; one of the many creatures who meet with Caspian at the Council at Dancing Lawn.

REALLY DEEP LAND (SC) (see BISM)

REDHAVEN (VDT) City on Brenn, one of the Seven Isles.

REEPICHEEP (VDT, PC, LB) Gallant and brave mouse, most valiant of all the Talking Beasts and Chief Mouse. (The mice ate Aslan's cords in LWW and became Talking Beasts.) About two-feet high, he wears a long crimson feather on his head and a long sword. Wounded in PC and healed by Lucy; his tail restored by Aslan. Sails on the "Dawn Treader" and is left in Aslan's country at World's End.

RESTIMAR (VDT) (see SEVEN LORDS)

REVILIAN (VDT) (see SEVEN LORDS)

RHINCE (VDT) Mate on the "Dawn Treader" who helps sail the ship with Drinian.

RHINDON (PC) Peter's sword, a gift from Father Christmas, with which he kills the wolf in LWW.

RHOOP (VDT) (see SEVEN LORDS)

RILIAN (SC) Son of Caspian X and Ramandu's daughter who seeks to avenge his mother's death by the green serpent. Enchanted by the Green Witch and rescued by children in SC.

RISHDA TARKAAN (LB) Calormene captain who helps Shift and Ginger the Cat plot against Aslan and Tirian; carried away by Tash.

RISHTI TARKAAN (HHB) Aravis's grandfather.

RIVER-GOD (PC, MN) Being who rises from the Great River at Beruna Bridge. Father of the Naiads.

ROGIN (HHB) Red Dwarf, one of Duffle's brothers.

ROONWIT (LB) Great golden-bearded centaur. Reads the stars and warns Tirian of danger over Narnia. His forces were supposed to join Tirian; he is killed by Calormene arrow but is seen in Aslan's country.

RUMBLEBUFFIN (LWW) Giant who helps Aslan fight the witch in LWW and borrows Lucy's tiny handkerchief. "Rumble" means to make a lot of noise; "Buffian" means buffoon (OED).

RUSH RIVER (PC) River that joins Great River at Beruna's Bridge.

RYNELF (VDT) Sailor on the "Dawn Treader."

SALAMANDERS (SC) Live in Bism in the fire-river. Small dragons, witty and eloquent. According to legend, salamanders, gnomes, sylphs, and nymphs inhabited fire, one of the four elements.

SALLOWPAD (HHB) Old and wise raven who is an advisor to Queen Susan and Edmund; always quotes pithy sayings. "Sallow" is yellow/brown.

SARAH (MN) Andrew's and Letty's housemaid.

SATYR (LWW, PC, SC, MN, LB) Woodland god that is part man and part goat.

SCRUBB (VDT) (see EUSTACE, ALBERTA, HAROLD). The name means "a person of little account and poor appearance, insignificant"; can also mean to scratch one's body (OED)—appropriate considering Eustace's original personality and the fact that he scratches at his dragonish scales. Lewis says he "half deserved" his name.

SEA GIRL (VDT) Fish-herdress Lucy sees near World's End. They become friends just by looking at each other. May illustrate kinship one can find in any world.

SEA PEOPLE (VDT) People riding sea horses, whom Lucy sees near the World's End. They wear no clothes, have ivory bodies, purple hair; wear coronets, pearls, gold on their foreheads and emerald and orange streamers on their shoulders. They are hunting for fish.

SEA SERPENT (VDT) Serpent that attacks the "Dawn Treader." Green and vermillion, with purple blotches, head like a horse, enormous eyes, fish teeth, and gigantic tail.

SEVEN BROTHERS OF THE SHUDDERING WOODS (PC) Red Dwarfs who live in an underground smithy and give armor to Caspian.

SEVEN FRIENDS OF NARNIA (LB) Digory, Polly, Peter, Lucy, Edmund, Eustace, and Jill.

SEVEN ISLES (PC) Islands, including Bren and Muil, visited by the "Dawn Treader."

SEVEN LORDS (VDT) Seven Telmarine lords of Caspian IX, sent by usurper Miraz to sail away searching for new lands beyond the Eastern Ocean. Caspian searches for them in VDT. Their names are as follows:

Argoz Found sleeping at Ramandu's Island. "Argos" means swift, a ship sailing on an adventurous voyage (like the Argonauts) (BDFM).

Revilian Found sleeping at Ramandu's Island.

Bern Found living on a Lone Island under Gumpas; Caspian makes him Duke. From "Berne/Beorn" meaning warrior, hero (OED).

Mavramorn Found sleeping at Ramandu's Island.

Octesian Either killed by dragon or was the dead dragon Eustace encountered.

Restimar Turned to gold on Deathwater Island.

Rhoop Found on Dark Island (where dreams come true). Allowed to recover in a restful sleep at Aslan's Table.

SHADOW-LANDS (LB) Aslan's designation for England because it is only a copy of the Real England in his country.

SHALLOW-LANDS (SC) Gnomes' name for the Witch's Underland beneath Narnia.

SHAR (HHB) Fights for King Lune against the Calormenes. Obsolete word for "share" (OED).

SHASTA (HHB) (see COR) "Shasta" is Cor's Calormene name and is similar to other Calormene words ("sh" sound). Probably based on Hindu word; "Shastri" is one who is learned, teaches (OED).

SHIFT (LB) West Narnian ape who persuades Puzzle to wear lion skin and masquerade as Aslan. Example of person who wishes to set up a socialistic state and/or false religion. Possible connection with word "shifty."

SHRIBBLE RIVER (SC, LB) East-West river near southern border of Ettinsmoor.

SILENUS (PC) Old man on donkey who accompanies Bacchus. In mythology, he was a drunken and jovial attendant of Bacchus who rode an ass (BDFM).

SILVAN (PC, MN) Woodland spirit.

SILVER SEA (VDT) Lily Lake near the End of the World.

SLINKEY (LB) Fox who fights on Calormene side in LB and is killed by Eustace; appropriate name.

SNOWFLAKE (SC) Green Witch's lovely white horse.

SONS OF ADAM AND DAUGHTERS OF EVE (LWW, PC, SC, MN, LB) Humans; Aslan's name for the children. The phrase is based on the Biblical concept of fallen man.

SOPESPIAN (PC) Traitor Telmarine lord of usurper Miraz who helps plan Miraz's defeat by tricking him into accepting challenge to duel. Peter kills him.

SORLOIS (MN) Dead world like Charn.

SPEAR-HEAD (VDT) North-star of Narnia, brighter than pole star.

SPIVVINS (SC) Lewis is not clear who or what this is. Eustace keeps a secret about Spivvins under torture at Experiment House.

SPLENDOUR HYALINE (HHB) Galleon ship (see HYALINE), the royal ship for the four Pevensie rulers.

"SPOTTY" SORNER (SC) One of the children at Experiment House. A "sorner" is one who sponges off people (OED).

STABLE HILL (LB) Location of the Stable where first Tash, then Aslan, are found. Its inside is bigger than its outside.

STARS (VDT, LB) Portrayed as real people, glimmering with silver clothes and hair. North American Indians believed that stars were people.

STONEFOOT (LB) Giant who is to be part of Tirian's troop in final battle but is never summoned.

STONE KNIFE (LWW, VDT) Knife of cruel and ancient shape used by Witch to kill Aslan. Kept by Ramandu at Aslan's Table. In VDT, the three lords touch it while arguing and fall into an enchanted sleep. Stone could be associated with Old Testament Law.

STONE TABLE (LWW, VDT) Table where Aslan is sacrificed. A slab of grey stone supported by four upright stones; old and covered with engraved lines and figures. Splits in two after the sacrifice. Later placed in central cave hollowed out within a mound built over it (Aslan's How). Stones are also important in ancient religions and *Till We Have Faces*. Lewis is most likely basing this on a rich pagan tradition. The fact that the table breaks in two is reminiscent of the veil being rent in two in the Temple during Christ's sacrifice.

STORMNESS HEAD (HHB) Mountain on the border of Narnia and Archenland.

STRAWBERRY (MN) (see FLEDGE)

SUNLESS SEA (SC) Sea that must be crossed in order to reach all outlets from Shallow Lands.

SUSAN PEVENSIE (LWW, HHB, PC) One of the four Pevensie children known for her beauty. Not allowed into Aslan's country because she is "no longer a friend of Narnia" and is interested only in superficial things.

SWANWHITE (LB) Queen who lived in Narnia before the days of the White Witch and the Great Winter. Was so beautiful that when she looked into any forest pool, the reflection of her face shone out of the water for a year and a day afterwards like a star by night.

TACKS (VDT) One of Gumpas' slave merchants.

TALKING BEASTS (MN, SC) Narnian animals given the gift of speech and dominion over Dumb Beasts.

TARKAAN (HHB) A great lord in Calormen; known by gold ring on arm.

TARKHEENA (HHB) A great lady in Calormen.

TARVA (PB) Planet; name means "Lord of Victory." Its conjunction with Alambil means good fortune for Narnia.

TASH (LB, HHB) Calormene god; its head is like an eagle or vulture, and it has four arms. "Tash" means blemish (OED). In *Till We Have Faces*, the priest of Ungit also wears a mask that makes him look like a bird. Tash requires human sacrifices (like Ungit in *TWHF*) and really exists, as evidenced in LB. Lewis is showing the reality of demons.

TASHBAAN (HHB, LB) Calormene city located on an island—one of the wonders of the world.

TASH-GOD (see TASH)

TASHLAN (LB) Shift's name for the false Aslan, an attempt to equate Aslan with Tash. An anti-Christ figure.

TEHISHBAAN (LB) Emeth's city, west beyond the desert.

TELMAR/TELMARINES (PC, VDT, HHB) Land beyond the western mountains. Discovered through a magic cave on an Island in the Southern Seas. After a famine, Caspian I King of Telmar led the people to the Western Mountains of Narnia and conquered it, silencing the beasts, trees, fountains, and driving away or killing the dwarfs and fauns. Because the Telmarines fear the Sea, they fabricate lies about ghosts residing in the Black Woods. They permit these lies to grow as a protection from the Sea. "Tel" has several meanings (endure, bear) but "mar" and "marine" obviously refer to the sea.

TEREBINTHIA (VDT, SC) Island visited by the "Dawn Treader" after Galma where there is a terrible sickness. Caspian seeks Aslan there in SC.

THORNBUT (HHB) Dwarf under King Edmund who orders Corin not to fight in the battle against the Calormenes.

TIRIAN (LB) Last ruler of Narnia, seventh in descent from Rilian; fights the final battle of Narnia. Name probably from "tire," meaning to fail, cease, diminish, give out (OED)—appropriate, since during his reign Narnia is destroyed.

TISROC (HHB) Ruler of Tashbaan.

TOMBS OF THE ANCIENT KINGS (HHB) Tombs north of Tashbaan that look like gigantic beehives; there are rumors of ghouls there. There Shasta spends the night and meets Aravis, Hwin, and Bree before their journey back to Narnia.

TRAN (HHB) Member of Archenland nobility who fights for King Lune against the Calormenes.

TREE OF PROTECTION (MN) Tree that grows from a seed of the silver apple Digory gets for his mother. The apple core from this tree planted in England eventually becomes the magic wardrobe.

TREE PEOPLE (PC) Trees in Narnia look like people when their residing spirits become visible. Retreat in New Narnia but are awakened again by Aslan in PC. Eat various kinds of soil and wade in the dirt. Birches, beeches, and larches are girls; oaks are shaggy, wizened, hearty men with frizzled beards; elms are lean and melancholy. Based on the dryads of mythology.

TRUFFLEHUNTER (PC, VDT, LB) Badger who first helps Caspian in his war against Miraz and later serves under him when Caspian becomes king. A "truffle" is a round, underground edible fungus or root (OED).

TRUMPKIN (SC, PC, VDT, LB) Nicknamed D.L.F. (Dear Little Friend). Red Dwarf who is Lord Regent under Caspian X. Tells children story of Caspian X and leads them to him at Aslan's How.

TUMNUS (LWW, HHB, LB) Faun who lives in a cave and befriends Lucy on her first solo trip to Narnia. Is turned into stone by the Witch for treachery. Appears again in HHB to plan way for Narnians to escape Tashbaan by feigning a party for Rabadash. Name reminiscent of "Tumulus," which is a mound of earth—appropriate since he lives in the ground (OED). Idea for LWW began with a picture in Lewis's mind of a faun carrying an umbrella.

TURKISH DELIGHT (LWW) Candy the White Witch uses to tempt Edmund. A jelly-like sweet flavored with flower essences, usually cut into cubes and covered in icing sugar.

UNDERLAND (SC) Land beneath Narnia inhabited by the Earthmen, who call it the Shallow-Lands.

UNICORN (LWW, LB) Legendary creature like a horse with one horn. Symbol of Christ and purity.

URNUS (SC) A faun.

UVILAS (PC) One of Caspian IX's lords who, under usurper Miraz, was intentionally shot with arrows at a hunting party.

VOLTINUS (PC) A faun who dances for Caspian X.

VOLUNS (PC) A faun who dances for Caspian X.

WATER RAT (LB) Rat on a river raft carrying logs from Narnia to sell to the Calormenes under Shift's orders. One of the first signs to alert Tirian that something is amiss in Narnia.

WER-WOLF (LWW, PC) One of Nikabrik's cohorts, brought to attack Aslan's group. Half man, half wolf.

WESTERN WILDS (LWW, PC, MN, LB) Area at far west of Narnia where Digory and Polly travel on the day Narnia is created. Wild land of mountains, dark forests, snow, and glaciers. Location of hill with garden and apple tree where final events in LB take place.

WHITE STAG (LWW, PC, HHB) Stag that would grant wishes if one caught him. The four children (Kings and Queens) hunt him at end of LWW and rediscover the lamp-post where they first entered Narnia.

WHITE WITCH (LWW, MN) (see JADIS)

WIMBLEWEATHER (PC) Giant of Deadman's Hill and part of Caspian's troops. Spoils Caspian's surprise attack on Miraz's army. "Wimble" means active, nimble (EDEL).

WINDING ARROW RIVER (HHB) East-west river between Archenland and Calormen.

WOOD BETWEEN THE WORLDS (MN) Beautifully quiet, rich and alive woodland where Digory and Polly end up with their magic rings. Contains dozens of pools that lead to other worlds.

WORLD'S END ISLAND (VDT) Island of Ramandu and Aslan's Table, so named because for those who sail from it, it is the beginning of the end.

WRAGGLE (LB) Satyr who fights on Calormene side in LB. The word means to struggle or resist (OED).

ZARDEENAH (HHB) "Lady of the Night," Calormene moon goddess. Damsels do service to her before they are married; they bid farewell to her and sacrifice to prepare for marriage.

A Note on the Names and Creatures

ANIMALS like moles, badgers, and squirrels have very descriptive names: Pattertwig (squirrel), Trufflehunter and Hardbiter (badgers). The names Hwin and Bree are based on horse sounds. Dogs speak in "doggy" language: "We'll help, we'll help, help, help. Show us how to help, show us how, how. How-how-how?"

CENTAURS are based on Greek mythology and are a race of creatures having the head, arms, and trunk of a man and the body and legs of a horse. In Narnia, they have both a man-stomach and horse-stomach, as well. They are portrayed as majestic and solemn, not easily made merry or angry; but when aroused, their anger is terrible. They are supposed to be prophets, stargazers, and healers and have names like Cloudbirth, Glenstorm, and Roonwit.

FAUNS are from Roman mythology, where they were deities having a man's body from the waist up and the horns, legs, and tail of a goat. In Narnia, they have reddish skin, too. Appropriately, they have Latin names: Dumnus, Girbius, Mentius, Nausus, Nimienus, Obentinus, Orruns, Oscuns, Tumnus, Urnus, Voltinus, Voluns.

DWARFS of at least two kinds live in Narnia: black and red. In Norse mythology, there were black and white dwarfs, and the black were usually evil and associated with the earth and metal craftsmanship. Red dwarfs in Narnia have names like Duffle, Rogin, Trumpkin, and Bricklethumb; Nikabrik, an evil dwarf, is a Black Dwarf.

OTHER CREATURES mentioned in the books are based on tradition or classical mythology:

BOGGLES: Hobgoblins.
DRYADS: Wood nymphs who live in trees and preside over woods.
NAIADS: Nymphs who preside over brooks, springs, fountains.
SATYRS: Wood gods or demons with the pointed ears, legs, and short horns of a goat, or tail of goat or horse; associated with Bacchus.
GHOULS: Evil spirits that rob graves.
HAGS: Evil spirits, usually female, associated with Furies and Harpies.
MINOTAURS: Half man, half bull.
OGRES: Man-eating giant monsters.
SPRITES: Elves or pixies.
UNICORNS: Usually white and resembling a horse with one horn in center of forehead, symbol for purity.
WRAITHS: Ghosts of dead people.

NARNIAN NAMES (of royalty) seem to have -ian endings (perhaps deriving from the name Aslan): Caspian, Rilian, Tirian, Drinian, Erlian.

ARCHENLAND NAMES are predominantly monosyllabic, and brothers have similar names: Nain, Lune (Kings): Dar/Darrin, Col/Colin, Cor/Corin (brothers).

CALORMENE NAMES have a Persian or Turkish ring to them: Tash, Tashbaan, Ahoshta, Tarkaan, Lasaraleen, Shasta, Rabadash, Ahoshta, Arsheesh, Ardeeb, Alimash (many "s" and "sh" sounds).

EXPERIMENT HOUSE children have derogatory names: Eustace Clarence Scrubb ("Scrubb" means "an insignificant person," and Lewis says he half deserved the name); Jackle (Jackal?), Sorner (meaning "sponger"), Winter*blott*.

Bibliography

Books By C. S. Lewis Referred to in Text

The Abolition of Man. N.Y.: Macmillan, 1965.

An Experiment in Criticism. N.Y.: Cambridge UP, 1961.

Christian Reflections. Ed. Walter Hooper. Grand Rapids: Eerdmans, 1967.

C. S. Lewis Letters to Children, ed. Lyle W. Dorsett and Marjorie Lamp Mead. N.Y.: Macmillan, 1985.

The Discarded Image. N.Y.: Cambridge UP, 1964.

God in the Dock. Ed. Walter Hooper. Grand Rapids: Eerdmans, 1970.

The Great Divorce. N.Y.: Macmillan, 1946.

"Introduction." *Phantastes and Lilith.* By George MacDonald. Grand Rapids: Eerdmans, 1964.

Letters of C. S. Lewis. Revised and Enlarged Edition. Ed. Walter Hooper. N.Y.: Harcourt, 1993.

Letters to Malcolm: Chiefly on Prayer. N.Y.: Harcourt, 1964.

Mere Christianity. N.Y.: Macmillan, 1943.

Miracles. N.Y.: Macmillan, 1974.

On Stories and Other Essays on Literature. N.Y.: Harcourt, 1982.

Out of the Silent Planet. N.Y.: Macmillan, 1970.

Perelandra. N.Y.: Macmillan, 1970.

Pilgrim's Regress. Grand Rapids: Eerdmans, 1976.

Preface to Paradise Lost. London: Oxford UP, 1977.

The Screwtape Letters. N.Y.: Macmillan, 1961.

Studies in Medieval and Renaissance Literature. London: Cambridge UP, 1966.

Surprised By Joy. N.Y.: Harcourt, 1955.

That Hideous Strength. N.Y.: Macmillan, 1970.

The Weight of Glory. Grand Rapids: Eerdmans, 1975.

They Stand Together: Letters of C. S. Lewis to Arthur Greeves (1914-1963). Ed. Walter Hooper. N.Y.: Macmillan, 1979.

Till We Have Faces. Grand Rapids: Eerdmans, 1974.

Books About the Chronicles of Narnia

Bustard, Ned. *The Chronicles of Narnia Comprehension Guide*. Veritas Press, n.d.

Ditchfield, Christin. *A Family Guide to Narnia: Biblical Truths in C.S. Lewis's the Chronicles of Narnia*. Wheaton: Crossway, 2003.

Ford, Paul F. *Companion to Narnia*. San Francisco: HarperSanFrancisco, 1994.

Lindskoog, Kathryn Ann. *Journey Into Narnia*. Pasadena: Hope, 1997.

Manlove, Colin. *The Chronicles of Narnia: The Patterning of a Fantastic World*. N.Y.: Twayne, 1993.

Schakel, Peter J. *Imagination and the Arts in C. S. Lewis: Journeying to Narnia and Other Worlds*. Columbia: U. of Missouri, 2002.

—— *Reading With the Heart: The Way Into Narnia*. Grand Rapids, Michigan: Eerdmans Publishing Company, 1979

Sibley, Brian. *The Land of Narnia: Brian Sibley Explores the World of C. S. Lewis*. N.Y.: HarperCollins, 1990.

Background on Lewis

Barfield, Owen. "Introduction." *Light On C. S. Lewis*. Ed. Jocelyn Gibb. London: Bless, 1965.

Green, Roger Lancelyn and Walter Hooper. *C. S. Lewis: A Biography*. N.Y.: Harcourt, 1974.

Hooper, Walter. *C. S. Lewis: A Companion & Guide*. N.Y: HarperCollins, 1996.

—— "Narnia: The Author, the Critics, and the Tale." *The Longing for a Form*. Ed. Peter Schakel. Kent State UP, 1977. 105-118.

—— *"Past Watchful Dragons": The Narnian Chronicles of C. S. Lewis*. N.Y.: Collier, 1979.

—— "Preface." *Christian Reflections*. By C. S. Lewis. Grand Rapids: Eerdmans, 1967. vii-xiv.

Schultz, Jeffrey D. and John G. West Jr., Ed. *The C. S. Lewis Readers' Encyclopedia*. Grand Rapids: Zondervan, 1998.

Other Authors Referred to in Text

Chesterton, G. K. *Orthodoxy*. N.Y.: Image Books, 1959.

Christopher, Joe R. "The Romances of Clive Staples Lewis." Diss. U. Oklahoma, 1969.

Hillegas, Mark R. *Shadows of Imagination*. Carbondale: S. Illinois UP, 1969.

King, Don. "Narnia and the Seven Deadly Sins." *Mythlore* 10 (Spring 1984): 14-19.

MacDonald, George. "The Fantastic Imagination." *The Gifts of the Child Christ* (Vol. 1). Ed. Glenn Sadler. Grand Rapids: Eerdmans, 1973.

—— *Phantastes and Lilith.* Grand Rapids: Eerdmans, 1964.

Tolkien, J. R. R. "On Fairy Stories." *The Tolkien Reader.* N.Y.: Ballantine, 1966.

Ward, Michael. "Why There are Seven Chronicles of Narnia," *Times Literary Supplement*, April 2, 2003.

Original Publication of the Chronicles of Narnia

The Horse and His Boy. London: Geoffrey Bles, 1954. N.Y.: Macmillan, 1954.

The Last Battle. London: The Bodey Head, 1956. N.Y.: Macmillan, 1956.

The Lion, the Witch and the Wardrobe. London: Geoffrey Bles, 1950. N.Y.: Macmillan, 1950.

The Magician's Nephew. London: The Bodley Head, 1955. N.Y.: Macmillan, 1955.

Prince Caspian. London: Geoffrey Bles, 1951. N.Y.: Macmillan, 1951.

The Silver Chair. London: Geoffrey Bles, 1953. N.Y.: Macmillan, 1953.

The Voyage of the "Dawn Treader." London: Geoffrey Bles, 1952. N.Y.: Macmillan, 1952.

Editions of the Chronicles of Narnia

Chronicles of Narnia Seven-Volume Boxed Set. HarperCollins, 1994 (hardback and paperback).

The Complete Chronicles of Narnia. HarperCollins, 1998 (hardback) and 2001 (paper).

The Chronicles of Narnia Box Set: Full-Color Collector's Edition. HarperTrophy, 2000.

Speciality Books & Products

Books

Gresham, Douglas. *The Narnia Cookbook: Narnian Food from C.S. Lewis's Chronicles of Narnia.* N.Y. HarperCollins, 1998.

Riordan, James. *A Book of Narnians: The Lion, the Witch, and the Others.* N.Y. HarperCollins, 1995

Narnia Solo Adventure Series. Berkley Publishing Group (Choose Your Own Adventure game books), 1988:
   Return to Deathwater (1)
   The Sorceress and the Book of Spells (2)
   Leap of the Lion (3)
   The Lost Crowns of Cair Paravel (4)
   Return of the White Witch (5)
   The Magician's Rings (6)
   Keeper of the Dreamstone (7)

World of Narnia (adapted from The Chronicles of Narnia). Illustrated by Deborah Maze. N.Y. HarperCollins, 1998:

   Aslan
   Aslan's Triumph
   Edmund and the White Witch
   Lucy Steps Through the Wardrobe
   The Wood Between the Worlds

Graphic Abridged Versions:

   The Lion, the Witch and the Wardrobe: A Graphic Novel. Abridged and illustrated by Robin Lawrie. HarperTrophy, 1995.

The Magician's Nephew: A Graphic Novel. Abridged and illustrated by Robin Lawrie. HarperTrophy, 1999.

The Narnia Trivia Book. N.Y. HarperCollins, 1999.

Wisdom of Narnia, by C. S. Lewis, Pauline Baynes. N.Y.: HarperCollins, 2001.

Other Products

The Narnia Journal (The World of Narnia) by C. S. Lewis. Mary Collier (Illustrator). HarperCollins, 1997.

The Narnia Paper Dolls: The Lion, the Witch and the Wardrobe Collection. N.Y.: HarperCollins, 1998.

The World of Narnia Advent Calendar. N.Y. HarperCollins, 1998.

Selected Audio and DVD

The Chronicles of Narnia, 3 DVD set, The BBC and Home Vision Entertainment, 2002.

The Chronicles of Narnia CD Box Set, HarperAudio, 2004.

The Chronicles of Narnia Radio Theatre Complete Set (19 CDs), 1999.

Web Sites

C.S. Lewis Foundation	http://www.cslewis.org
C.S. Lewis Classics (HarperCollins site)	http://www.cslewis.com
Into the Wardrobe: The C. S. Lewis Web Site	http://cslewis.drzeus.net
Lindentree: Voyage to Narnia (Kathryn Lindskoog's site)	http://www.lindentree.org/voyage.html
Narnia Fans	http://www.narniafans.com/
NarniaMUCK	http://www.narnia.godscreations.net/
New York C.S. Lewis Society	http://www.nycslsociety.com
Virtual Narnia	http://www.virtualnarnia.com/
Welcome to Narnia (Walden Media site)	http://www.narnia.com/

Index

brightness 137
Bromious 192
Buffin 192
Bulgy Bears 192
Burnt Island 39, 192

C

dwarfs 46, 144, 197, 219

E

Earthmen 42, 79
Easter 161
Eastern Sea 197
Edith Jackle 197
Edith Winterblott 197
Edmund Pevensie 32, 105–107, 118, 142, 145, 153, 155, 157, 158,
    160, 162, 197
education 117
efreet 197
Eleanor Blakiston 197
Emeth 45, 46, 138, 146, 197
Emperor-Over-Sea 159, 197
End of the World 74, 175, 180
Erimon 197
Erlian 198
Ettins 198
Ettinsmoor 42, 198
Eucatastrophe 184
Eustace Scrubb 38, 41, 68, 107–109, 110, 154, 162, 181, 198
  undragoned 39, 94, 162
evil 60, 153–158
  discerning 157
Experiment House 19, 41, 43, 87, 109, 116, 117, 142, 144, 198, 219

F

fairy tale 23, 52, 91
faith 104, 142, 145, 146
false gods 156
Farsight 198
Father Christmas 106, 114, 198
Father Time 42, 46, 178, 198
fauns 198, 218
Felimath 38, 198
Felinda 198
Fenris Ulf 33, 199
film 47
fireberry 165
Fledge 31, 99, 143, 148, 199

Frank 31, 80, 81
free will 142

G

Gale 199
Galma 199
games 49
garden 99, 162, 181, 182, 183
Garden of Gethsemane 160
Garrett twins 199
gates 150
Genesis 148
gentle giants 199
geography 73
ghouls 199, 219
Ginger the Cat 45, 157, 199
Girbius 199
Glasswater Creek 199
Glenstorm 200
Glimfeather 41, 200
Glozelle 37, 200
gnomes 200
Golden Age 71
Goldwater 200
Golg 43, 173, 200
good book 125
good characters 133
Grahame, Kenneth 19
Grail legend 137
Grand Vizier 200
Great Desert 200
Great River 200
Great Sea 74
Great Snow Dance 43, 59
Great Story 186
Great Waterfall 181, 200
Great Woods 160, 200
greed 153, 155
Green, Roger Lancelyn 23, 25
Green Serpent 41
Green Witch 42, 63–64, 147, 153, 156, 158, 173
Gresham, Douglas 25, 29, 49

Jinn 61
joy 17
judgment 178

K

Kidrash 202
Kirke 19, 32, 66, 72, 100, 172, 174
Kirkpatrick 19

L

Lady Liln 203
Lady of the Green Kirtle 42, 203
Lamb 40, 134
lamp-post 36, 62, 75, 203
Lantern Waste 44, 62, 75, 203
Lapsed Bear of Stormness 203
Lasaraleen 35, 112, 203
Last Battle 44–49, 104, 109, 143, 156, 158, 169, 175, 181
Lefay, Mrs. 203
LeFay Fragment 24
Letty Ketterley 203
Lewis, C. S.
biography 15–20
  conversion 20
  writing the Narnia books 21–25
light 137, 180
Lilith 203
Lilygloves 203
lion 131, 132, 136
Lion, the Witch and the Wardrobe 22, 32–34, 67, 153, 184
Lone Islands 204
longing 17, 168–170
Lucy Pevensie 32, 102–104, 118, 140, 145, 147, 154, 160, 181, 204
Lune 35, 113, 204

M

Mabel Kirke 204
MacDonald, George 19, 20, 55, 129
Macmillan 29
Macready 204
Magdalen College 19

T

U

A Guide Through Narnia

Printed in the United States
40668LVS00007B/112

9 781573 833080